Breath of Relief

Transforming Compassion Fatigue into Flow

Breath of Relief

Transforming Compassion Fatigue into Flow

Karl LaRowe, MA, LCSW

Published by Acanthus Publishing
www.AcanthusPublishing.com

Published 2005 by Acanthus Publishing
a division of The Ictus Initiative

Library of Congress Cataloging-in-Publication Data

LaRowe, Karl.
    Breath of relief : transforming compassion fatigue into flow / by Karl LaRowe.
    p. cm.
    Includes bibliographical references.
    ISBN 0-9754810-2-9

    1. Post-traumatic stress disorder--Treatment. 2. Healing. 3. Qi gong. 4. Tai chi. I. Title.

RC552.P67L37 2005   616.85'21
                                                     QBI05-800205

Printed in the United States of America
10 9 8 7 6 5 4 3 2 1

Design | Charisse L. Brookman
Illustrations | Tom Gallagher
DVD production | Sean Mackie of Mack Media Productions

This book is dedicated to my Qigong Sifu,
Master Simon Yong, the man who helped
me to "glimpse the Tao."

Table of Contents:

Introduction:

A Crisis in Caregiving

Caring people sometimes experience pain as a direct result of their exposure to others' traumatic material. Unintentionally and inadvertently, this secondary exposure to trauma may cause helpers to inflict additional pain on the originally traumatized. This situation — call it Compassion Fatigue, Compassion Stress, or Secondary Traumatic Stress — is the natural, predictable, treatable, and preventable unwanted consequence of working with suffering people.

— B. Hudnall Stamm, *Secondary Traumatic Stress,* page 4

"I know I'm burned out," a recent participant in my Compassion Fatigue seminar told me. "I don't have any energy or enthusiasm as a social worker anymore. The strange thing is, when I get home from work I can't go to sleep. No matter how tired I feel I can't seem to turn my mind off. I can stare at the T.V. for hours, but all I see are the faces of patients I didn't have the time or energy to help. All I want to do anymore is just go numb…."

A great and growing crisis exists in caregiving. Healthcare professionals, from nurses and social workers in hospitals to counselors and staff in nursing homes, are experiencing more stress and burnout than ever before. Healthcare professionals are being called upon to give more of themselves to help others, particularly since the national trauma of September 11th, 2001. More of their time, energy, attention, and intention have been called upon to help alleviate the pain and suffering of others. Generally speaking, the response within the professional health care community has been consistent with the caregiving personality — doctors, nurses, psychologists, and a whole host of others have given, and given, and given.

Although the events of September 11 and the ongoing "War on Terror" have certainly placed an immediate and additional strain on healthcare providers — particularly those who work with trauma survivors — the healthcare industry has been facing its own crisis for a number of years. We've seen a significant shortage of staff and a significant rise in the number of people to be helped. According to a "60 Minutes" investigation reported on June 9, 2002 there are currently 120,000 open nursing positions nationwide with 400,000 positions expected to become vacant in the next 20 years, indicating that we're facing a widening gap between the number of patients and the qualified staff available to give them respite. This means more patients per nurse and less time and energy per patient.

Nursing isn't the only profession within the healthcare industry to experience this kind of strain. Social workers, psychologists, mental health therapists, case managers, and residential care facility workers are just a few of the other care providers who are also undergoing a similar dramatic increase in stress levels due to professional overload, arriving at work, day in and day out, to face increasing caseloads of severely physically, emotionally, and mentally ill patients accompanied by diminishing resources.

One of the results of this kind of increasing care provider stress is Compassion Fatigue. Compassion Fatigue is the result of unconsciously internalizing and freezing traumatic emotion (*Energy in MOTION*) into the very cells of your body as body memory. As one participant in one of my workshops put it "I can feel myself getting heavier as the week goes by. It's as though I'm carrying more and more of the weight of my caseload, the paperwork, and even my organization on my neck and shoulders each day. By Friday I'm so tense in my neck I can barely move my head."

Compassion Fatigue is secondary traumatic stress. It's often, although not exclusively, experienced by healthcare professionals who work with physically, psychologically, or emotionally traumatized patients and it has the tendency to manifest as disturbances in information processing similar to some of those reported by patients with Post Traumatic Stress Disorder (PTSD).

Compassion Fatigue presents a crisis in caregiving; like the Chinese character for crisis indicates, the current situation signifies both danger and opportunity.

The danger is clear and present. With the increasing caseloads and diminishing resources mentioned above, care providers are required to "multi-task." Translated into caregiver experience this often means more time and energy spent on crisis stabilization, documentation, and resource allocation with less spent on education and long-term management, resulting in risk management rather than health management. This shift of priorities is frustrating and exhausting, and it renders us more susceptible to unconsciously absorbing and internalizing the "frozen" energy of secondary trauma.

In the midst of the danger, though, opportunity exists, sometimes not as clear, but definitely present: Compassion Fatigue can be transformed into flow. Flow is a condition of mind and body that we experience when the mind and body become so connected that we get lost "in the zone." In a state of flow, you obtain such a sense of focus on the task at hand, because the task and your ability to do that task are so aligned, that external negativity and self-consciousness become irrelevant.

When the frozen energy of Compassion Fatigue is absorbed and internalized one of two things can happen. Either the energy accumulates and exacerbates Compassion Fatigue, or the energy is discharged through conscious breathing and mindful movement, activities that transform "energy residue" into flow and peak performance.

Healthcare professionals are uniquely positioned to experience flow in their daily work, creating a win-win situation for the caregiver and the patient. By learning to flow rather than freeze, healthcare professionals can transform the frozen energy of traumatic stress into synergy, harmony, and peak performance, traits that can be utilized to combat the expanding caseloads.

In my seminar "Transforming Compassion Fatigue Into Flow and Peak Performance," I share three basic governing principles of the Healer-Warrior philosophy, a paradigm that aligns the insights of martial arts with the research and scientific outlook of professional caregiving. Self-honesty, personal responsibility, and self-expression are the essential aspects we must possess in order to heal others, and each of these principles contain elements essential to the process of personal transformation.

Self-honesty is the key. It's the primary, essential process that allows a depth of access into parts of your personal self that can't be attained any other way.

In this context, self-honesty means self-transparency, the ability to look inward to cultivate "in-sight." Self-honesty is both a process and a skillful activity that can be learned and nurtured.

Most essential to developing self-honesty is the ability to suspend judgment, to halt the automatic response of immediately categorizing a concept or idea according to an already existing category of what may be right or wrong, good or bad, possible or impossible. This suspension isn't an easy thing to do; it requires a courageous willingness. Since most people rely on unquestioned beliefs to make sense of an unpredictable, often traumatic world, temporarily letting go of your belief systems can cause you to feel uneasy, even lost.

Unquestioned beliefs, the basic ideas we hold onto that become stagnant or outdated over time, can have remarkable powers to shape our perception by creating expectations within us that we project onto the external world. What we feel and think is selected and shaped to a great extent by what we unconsciously *expect* to experience.

As you read the words written in this book, try to utilize as much courageous transparency as possible, becoming aware of and suspending your unquestioned beliefs. Look intently inside yourself. Resist the temptation to immediately judge and classify the ideas shared before you have the chance to "try them on."

Personal responsibility is the continual willingness to take ownership of personal experience. The problem we usually run into with personal responsibility is our reluctance to surrender the *need to be right*.

The need to be right is one of our strongest and most strongly defended intentions, mainly because it supports and enforces the ego-illusion that I alone am special, different, and somehow more entitled than others. It's the basis of our misguided concept of what it means to be independent.

Personal responsibility is the degree of our willingness to take both individual and collective ownership for perceptions, thoughts, beliefs, emotions, and behaviors; communication with self and others; all relationships; and the conditions of life that we're now experiencing. This is not self-blame. To blame yourself you must split yourself into both the part that blames and the part that's getting blamed, an action that weakens your sense of self and distorts your perception of others.

Acting on personal responsibility means looking, listening, and letting go. It means practicing the art of surrendering, learning to give in without giving up, accepting the reality of a situation as it is without meeting the ego's demand to be right. Surrendering brings ego-perception more into alignment with the here and now, in-the-moment body experience.

Self-expression is the magic of transformation. When you become clear and open to intuitive signals, the music of the Natural Self, you'll begin to experience a deep sense of enjoyment and empowerment, a dance of energy and enjoyment that we all experience when we feel comfortable enough to let the Natural Self play.

The Natural Self is that place of connection between mind, body, Energy in *MOTION*, intuition, and insight that's in a constant state of flow. It's both in the heart and from the heart; it's a wise, gentle, powerful, and playful being inside each of us that's usually invisible to the ego's eye. The Natural Self lives in the heart, perceiving the world in terms of "us," while the ego resides in the head, thinking only of "me." The Natural Self senses connection and commonality while the ego notices separation and specialness.

Self-expression becomes the action of clearly tuning into the music of the Natural Self and allowing that music to move you, moment to moment, as you dance in ever-growing harmony and synchrony. Self-expression is the spontaneous alignment of who you are with what you're doing.

As you read this book, remember to relax your shoulders and breathe fully from your diaphragm. Allow a sense of connection and flow between your head and heart to develop so that you can listen to yourself with your intuition as well as your conscious mind. Allow yourself to become immersed while observing, moment to moment, what's happening in your body and mind as you dance in harmony and empowerment with your Natural Self.

Chapter One:

The Caregiving Personality

Trauma can teach the art of empathy, the ability to experience heart-to-heart what another person is feeling. This same set of experiences can render us more vulnerable, though; it can lead to unconsciously absorbing and internalizing, as secondary traumatic stress, the freezing cold fear that our clients experience in their own bodies and minds.

Introduction

Care providers are unique people. We have the gift of being able to connect with others in ways that are difficult to explain and even more difficult for others to understand. Our unique ability to join emotionally with our clients, an ability that allows us a near first-hand experience of a client's inner world, is perhaps our greatest gift; it's also our greatest challenge.

I often ask participants in my Compassion Fatigue workshop how many of them knew they were going to be caregivers before they reached college. A consistent 50 to 60 percent of the participants raise their hands. When asked what percentage of healthcare providers who specialize in work with traumatized clients were exposed to childhood trauma, most participants say they believe it's between 75 and 90 percent.

It's really no mystery that people who share certain traumatic life experiences would choose the path of professional caregivers as a way of making some positive use out of those experiences. Trauma can teach the art of empathy, the ability to experience heart-to-heart what another person is feeling. This same set of experiences can render us more vulnerable, though; it can lead to unconsciously absorbing and internalizing, as secondary traumatic stress, the freezing cold fear that our clients experience in their own bodies and minds.

Personality and Profession

Those of us who took the Strong-Campbell Vocational Interest Inventory (that long, boring test that tells us what we're supposed to be when we grow up) will recognize it as a type of personality test. Its validity is based upon years of trials that show a strong correlation between basic personality styles and the kinds of jobs those styles are drawn to. Some of the personality traits that attracted us to caregiving as a profession are wonderfully altruistic, but they can also carry with them some darker consequences, rendering us vulnerable to stress, burnout, and depression.

Most of us are drawn to the profession of caregiving, no matter what specific job we take. We're drawn by the desire to be of service to other people, by strong emotions and beliefs, and by the burning need to understand how and why people think, feel, and behave the way they do. Take a moment and reflect for yourself. Why did you become a care provider? Did you find the career, or did it seem to find you?

Dr. Paul Pearsall in his book *The Heart's Code* identifies several personality traits that he calls "cardio-sensitive" and describes them as unique to people who are more "tuned in" to the subtle energies of the heart. I believe care providers share a number of these traits, such as:

1. A Feminine Point of View

One of the core competencies in all areas of professional health care is the ability to develop and maintain empathy, a trait that's been traditionally viewed as feminine. Empathy is the basis for interpersonal and intra-personal intelligence. Women are often culturally identified as having a greater facility to intuit and creatively respond to other people's feelings. Dr. Daniel Goleman in his book *Emotional Intelligence* reports that "In tests with over seven thousand people in the United States and eighteen other countries, the benefits of being able to read feelings from non-verbal cues included being better adjusted emotionally, more popular, more outgoing, and — perhaps not surprisingly — more sensitive. In general, women are better than men at this kind of empathy."[1]

But that doesn't mean that empathy, despite being a feminine trait, is corralled in only one gender. Both men and women in the health care profession have a tendency to exhibit an extraordinary ability to connect with others on a very subtle emotional level. According to research psychologist Carol Gilligan, as reported in *The Heart's Code,* professional caregivers "take on a more collective orientation based on caring connection."[2]

2. An Ability to Remain Open-Minded

Dr. Pearsall notes that the most cardio-sensitive people he interviewed were "accommodators rather than assimilators,"[3] meaning

---

[1] Daniel Goleman, *Emotional Intelligence,* page 97

[2] Paul Persall, *The Heart's Code,* page 95

[3] *Ibid,* page 95

that they revised already existing paradigms for thinking about the world around them.

One of the real pleasures in providing workshops is the opportunity to interact with large numbers of healthcare professionals who I've found to be, for the most part, open to new ideas, interested in the new research, and who very often will point me in directions I'd never considered. Most of the people I've worked with have been willing to wait before they judge, experimented with new thoughts and procedures, and exhibited a fluid frame of mind, rather than a rigid and narrow outlook that confines them to one way of thinking.

To be open-minded you must have a willingness to suspend judgment, to courageously step outside the parameters of our scientifically-culturally biased perceptions and look at yourself from a new and fresh perspective. Real open-mindedness requires the ability to look at yourself with the same clarity and transparency you use when observing others, and I've seen this trait in action when working with fellow health care providers, from nurses to psychologists.

3. A Strong Sense of Body Awareness

Body awareness is the ability to place your attention inside your body and to sense and feel the connection every part of you has with every other part.

Care providers tend to fall into two fairly distinct groups: those who have done considerable work on and in their bodies, and those who tend to be somewhat disconnected from their physical being. A considerable number of social workers, nurses, and counselors who come to my seminars on Compassion Fatigue are very experienced in some form of body oriented therapy or physical exercise. Even before current research suggested the importance of a mind/body approach to working with trauma survivors, these survivor-helpers were intuitively tuned to their bodies. Any honest and persistent pursuit in self-healing will lead a survivor at some point back to the body.

The other set of care providers, those who appear somewhat disconnected from their physical being, still often manage to maintain a curiosity about a mind/body approach despite the disconnect. Usually the physical dissociation isn't due to lack of interest, but lack of time. Their personal and professional lives are just too hectic, too chaotic, and they don't have the time or energy to pay attention to their actual, physical existence.

4. A High Degree of Creativity

Traumatic stress often works as a curb to creativity. It results in physical and emotional constriction that's expressed as an almost deadly seriousness, a state of mind that's an anticipation of pain. When we feel safe enough to explore new ideas, though, particularly if we're engaged in teamwork, everyone can be tremendously creative. I've noticed health care providers to be even more so. Dr. Ellen Langer in her book *Mindfulness* finds creativity to be an essential quality of mindfulness, a state of being fully aware, fully conscious of the body and the world. She explains that "Many, if not all, of the qualities that make up a mindful attitude are characteristic of creative people. Those who can free themselves of old mindsets, who can open themselves to new information and surprise, play with perspective and context, and focus on process rather than outcome are likely to be creative whether they are scientists, artists, or cooks."[4]

Creativity is a condition of the Natural Self. When you feel "safe enough" and "good enough" in your body and your environment, the Natural Self will come out to play. The willingness to play with new ideas, perceptions, and perspectives is the core of creativity.

5. An Advanced Ability to Engage in Visualization

I've experienced caregivers to be highly capable of creating an internal, mental vision of possible realities, but this type of visualization can be a double-edged sword. We can use directed visualization to consciously form our experience, purposefully imaging a positive outlook in our consciousness and then using that "insighted mindset" to guide us through the day. Unconscious visualization, on the other hand, can often lead to images and thoughts of what we dislike or fear, negatively affecting our outlook.

The use of directed imagery in visualization has been studied and utilized extensively in sports psychology. In the book *Applied Sport Psychology: Personal Growth to Peak Performance,* contributing author Robin S. Vealey explains that "evidence supporting the positive

---

[4] Ellen Langer, *Mindfullness,* page 115

influence of imagery on sport performance is impressive. Both scientifically controlled studies and experiential accounts of the use of imagery to enhance performance report positive results."[5]

The same visualizing techniques that get applied to sports can be applied more generally to enhance everyday performance of any activity. Visualization is more than directed imaging; it includes the use of memory fragments (both implicit and explicit), body motion, emotional or affective charging, and cognitive mapping. In this way, the conscious visualization can unite the body and mind into one unit, creating a combined physical and mental reality.

In the end, visualization is inevitable; we either visualize with conscious intent, or unconsciously (and usually negatively) by default. When consciously directed visualization is performed utilizing multi-sensory rehearsal, the enhancement of performance and enjoyment is significant. When visualization is done by default, we most often visualize that which we fear. It's the same mechanism behind a "self-fulfilling prophecy."

6. Compulsive, Dependant Behavior, or Unresolved Grief

These personality traits, which are very consistent with Compassion Fatigue, often develop as a result of the traumatic experiences many care providers have experienced in their lives. As noted before, traumatic personal experiences can be the wellspring of empathy and wisdom; they can also result in unresolved grief that's often expressed as dependency and compulsive behavior.

One common personality trait of care providers is our tendency toward compulsiveness. This can actually be a valued trait sought out by managers and supervisors, something I can attest to as a former clinical director and program manager. Having employees who were somewhat rigid about completing tasks and taking a high degree of responsibility for their work is a great thing on the job. This trait, however, can also result in burnout, especially when combined with emotional dependency and unresolved grief.

The trauma or significant loss in the lives of many care providers can linger. It's no mystery that a number of us have, do, or will experience major depression that often requires medication and therapy. Dr. Pearsall finds that cardio-sensitive people, a term that we can associate with empathic care providers, "had experienced what they described and family members confirmed as a 'severe break' in a prior emotional bond. Many reported an especially

difficult divorce or the premature loss of a parent, which still plagued them emotionally even after several years had passed. There seemed to be a chronic, mildly depressive nature sometimes masked by self-depreciating humor."[6]

Dependency, like compulsivity, is often the result of trauma left hanging, of scarring events that have taken root in the body's mind as "need-desire," a desire or want that's experienced with the same intensity and tenacity as an unmet basic need, as an "emotional hunger" that mirrors physical hunger. It can draw our attention and intention inward toward its constantly aching emptiness.

As one counselor who works with battered women told me, "I never imagined that unresolved grief could actually affect how and where I would be drawn to find work. The fact is I'm most fulfilled when I'm able to consciously work on some of my own dependency issues while being of service to other women with similar issues." When we have unresolved issues in our own lives, they can appear, again and again, in unconscious ways as we work with the pain of others. As a way of dealing with our own trauma, we can become scrupulous to the point of compulsion and even succumb, sometimes, to an overwhelming need to be needed.

7. A Sensual Attunement and an Ability to Dream and Flow

This last set of personality traits speaks to our capacity to engage the Natural Self in spontaneous and playful creative flow, to find ourselves experiencing the condition of alignment and synchrony between mind, body, and Energy in MOTION that results in higher levels of satisfaction and performance.

Sensuality in this context refers to being in touch with your physical self from the inside out. It's the ability to delight in the experience of physical touch as well as sense that sweet place where physical and emotional energies intertwine and circulate throughout the body and mind. Sensuality dances in the heart of the Natural Self.

The dreamer is the playful, imaginative, child-like self that we often tell to "stand still and be quiet" as we attend to our important, serious, adult work. The dreamer is the flowing, unformed, creative

---

[5] Robin S. Vealey, "Imagery Training for Performance Enhancement" in
  Applied Sport Psychology: Personal Growth to Peak Performance, page 209

[6] Paul Persall, *The Heart's Code,* page 97

impulse that's just below the surface of consciousness. It's waiting, always ready to come out and play.

To flow is to consciously engage the sensual dreamer in playful, creative activity. Flow is the result of surrendering to the present moment and aligning who you are with what you're doing in spontaneous action.

Repeating and Remembering

Sigmund Freud said, "You will repeat instead of remember." I believe he was talking about the repetition compulsion, or the tendency in some clients to compulsively repeat patterns of behavior rather than remember their origins, often in an attempt to "master the stimulus retrospectively." Bessel A. Van der Kolk, in the book *Traumatic Stress,* calls it "compulsive re-exposure," and writes that "One set of behaviors that is not mentioned in the diagnostic criteria for PTSD is the compulsive re-exposure of some traumatized individuals to situations reminiscent of the trauma… In this reenactment of the trauma, an individual may play the role of either victimizer or victim."[7]

In some ways, care providers may compulsively re-expose themselves at work to the very same kind of trauma that they experienced at home earlier in their lives. One care provider at a recent workshop told me "I didn't realize it at the time, but the very same conditions of danger and unpredictability that characterized my childhood home environment were also some of the same conditions as my last job." The tendency to repeat patterns of trauma through compulsive re-exposure is one of the major psychological mechanisms at work in Compassion Fatigue. The re-exposure may be in the form of working with survivors who experienced a trauma similar to ours, or working in an emotionally toxic environment with unpredictable rules and relationships.

I've recognized the tendency to repeat the past in myself, and can attest to the fact that such recognition can be hard won. As a survivor therapist just out of graduate school, I was initially drawn to crisis intervention in a very busy emergency room. As I look back on it now, I realize I was drawn to the chaos, unpredictability, and even danger in a job position that was brand new and not well

formulated, with little definition or boundaries, a perfect repetition of my family of origin with all of the dramatic relationships that would eventually play out. It took me years to realize that I was putting myself back into the chaotic place I thought I'd left.

Re-exposure to personal trauma by working with clients who experienced trauma similar to ours is one of the most direct ways care providers can reactivate their own frozen-in-fear body memory as well as absorb and internalize the emotions of their clients. Emotion really is *Energy* in *MOTION*. As care providers empathically attune their receiving hearts to the frequency of their clients' sending hearts, that energy stamp is recorded in the receivers' hearts and bodies. When the energy received is felt to be familiar in its tone and frequency, a sympathetic response may develop, resulting in absorption and internalization of that energy.

The situation that's more difficult to identify is when re-exposure to personal, individual, and collective trauma manifests in working relationships with co-workers, supervisors, and in organizations. The places of occupation, or even the groups within that place, can have a profound effect on the therapists hired and on internal relationships. Personal and collective patterns of perception, reaction, and inaction can and do form as a result of dynamics that can be re-enacted in relationships at work. It may be as simple as consciously or unconsciously, with intent or with inertia, we bring who we are to what we do and who we do it with.

---

[7] Bessel A. Van der Kolk, A.C. McFarlane, and L. Weisaeth (eds), *Traumatic Stress,* page 10

Empathy is the process of developing rapport through emotional attunement, the ability to intuit another person's feelings and read non-verbal channels.

Empathy and Sympathy

The core competence for all care providers and all caregiving is the capacity for, and the ability to develop, empathy, defined by the Oxford American dictionary as "The ability to identify oneself mentally with a person or things and so understand his feelings or its meaning."

Empathy is the process of developing rapport through emotional attunement, the ability to intuit another person's feelings and read non-verbal channels. In a way, empathy sets in motion the internal mental and emotional conditions necessary to still your mind, suspend judgment, and listen with your heart and gut. It's a fundamental therapeutic skill that allows you to become a "participant-observer" during the process of communicating with your client. The participant part of you, your feeling-intuitive side, joins with your clients by developing a connection with them. The observer part of you detaches without disconnecting from the content of what occurs and is able to clearly and objectively observe the process of your transactions with your client as they unfold. The participant-observer watches, feels, and experiences from *inside* the body as well as attending to what transpires outside.

The art of cultivating a helping relationship depends on the ability to join, intuit, move, and mirror another person's emotion. This ability involves simultaneously "hovering" in the transaction zone while you observe, process, and respond to the unfolding of the interaction between yourself and your client. It's the dance of flow between care provider and client.

Empathy and sympathy are closely related terms. So what's the difference between empathy and sympathy and how do you know which one you're feeling?

First, there's no clear dividing line between the subtle energies of empathy and sympathy, just because we need one to draw differences. In most concepts in the human services field there's no clear dividing line; divisions and separations are self-induced because we believe the divisions in our thinking will provide more clarity. Actually, they produce more confusion. It's probably closer to the truth that we apply a different mix of empathy and sympathy to each person or situation we focus our attention on.

There is, however, a useful guideline to noticing when your empathy/sympathy mix may be out of balance. One of my professors many years ago advised me to "listen to the music and not just the words." The participant part of you is the part that's open and receptive to the "music" of your client. The observer listens to the words, it's that part of you that's detached, not disconnected, from the "pull" of the emotional interchange while clearly and objectively observing the content and process of your transactions as they unfold.

The emergence of an out-of-balance sympathetic response occurs when your client, coworker, or supervisor says something that draws in your observing self, causing you to lose your connection with the "being" inside your body. Rather than noticing how the emotion is experienced inside your body, you *become* the emotion. Rather than observing from a viewing point you're now engulfed and locked into your point of view. Being right begins to become more important than being clear.

In one of my first seminars on Compassion Fatigue an insightful social worker who works primarily with borderline personality disorders told me "I know I've taken the bait and gotten hooked by my client when the focus of my attention, my central awareness, suddenly changes, from a wide-angle, flowing perspective to a tight, narrow, constricted beam. And always, I begin to tighten my neck and shoulders and restrict my breath." When our observing part becomes overly engaged, we lose ourselves in our client's emotions and become physically and mentally fixed into a state that can result in countertransference.

Countertransference

Countertransference is a term that's often used, and misused, in describing some of the sensations, feelings, and emotions experienced by the caregiver in response to his or her empathic or sympathetic connection with the client. Confusion in the session often develops when we're unable or unwilling to distinguish our own reactions to past personal traumas from our clients'. Sensations, feelings, and emotions associated with past trauma become reactivated as the result of an empathic connection with the client.

The Care Provider's Physical/Affective/Ideational Response to His or Her Client

It's a good idea to get in touch with your personal sense of physical-emotional being, where most of the action takes place.

As you'll discover in the chapter on parallel process, human beings are actually much more connected than we like to believe. One of the best ways for me to know what's transpiring with my client is to listen with my own "felt-sense" to what is simultaneously transpiring in my own body, emotions, thoughts, and images.

When we sit and listen to our clients we receive energy as well as information. It's inevitable. We can, will, and do absorb the emotions of our clients.

Becoming body aware makes you more sensitive to your own internal movement of energy, sensations, affects, various tension levels, and, most importantly, breathing. When you maintain this awareness, you're more able to identify which physical and emotional sensations are responding to what your client is describing to you, allowing you to separate the client-caused reactions from those arising from your own personal history.

In addition to the body/emotional response to countertransference, there's also the ideational and information processing response. "Ideational" refers to the content of information your brain processes, content that can present itself as thoughts or ideas, sounds, visual images, and memory fragments. Fear is the emotion most often associated with such content, though. This gives most ideational content the power to intrude upon the screen of our conscious mind or be projected unconsciously onto others.

The Therapist's Conscious and Unconscious Defenses

The immediate, *conscious* physical and emotional response to another person with whom we have an empathic connection and who is experiencing fear and pain, especially if our own body-mind is attuned to that particular kind of pain or fear, is to freeze.

We generally freeze up along with the client, even if the freeze is something as subtle as holding or restricting breath throughout the session. How many times have you come gasping for air out of an intensive interview with a client? The first physical response to the experience of fear, yours or that of your client, is to hold your breath.

In addition to holding your breath, you'll also feel an acute or chronic muscle tension, usually in the neck, shoulders, and back. This hardened tension results from constantly squeezing your shoulders up and in. This is the body's frozen-in-fear-like-a-statue stance.

Countertransference and Unconscious Projection

Allow yourself to be as honest and transparent as possible and look out into the world from a very still and quiet place within the center of your body/mind. Notice what really gives shape, form, and color to what you "see." A great deal of what you actually physically perceive, and most of what you notice or pay attention to, has been created by the projection or transferring of your own personal reality onto the screen of your perception of others and the "world out there."

Certain countertransference reactions can be a type of projection that's usually unconscious and develops between care provider and client, resulting in the provider perceiving the client as either a mirror of the provider's idealized self, or as the "paranoid object," the devalued other.

In a mirroring countertransference, the care provider primarily sees the client as an extension of the provider's own narcissistic self. In this way, the client is perceived and valued to the extent that he or she is seen to share with the caregiver certain common experiences, values, preferences, coping styles, etc. The caregiver can become quite taken with the client personally and begin to lose the observer self as he or she participates more fully in mirroring, and being mirrored by, the client.

The flip side to a mirroring countertransference is the devaluation of the client by depositing the unwanted, unworthy, disowned parts of the care provider's self onto the screen of the client. The client becomes the receptacle for the caregiver's persecutory self-representations, the "paranoid object."

In both types of countertransference, the care provider unconsciously attempts to maintain emotional balance and self-consolidation by over-identifying with traits he or she perceives as positive that become projected onto the person of the client and splitting off and disowning traits experienced to be bad or contaminated.

When Wanting Feels Like Needing

When our desire to be seen and heard is mutated by our need to be right, needed, important, or special, we experience a state called "need-desire," a state I touched on previously. For care providers, our need-desire to be right or special can trap us in the compulsion to give more of ourselves to our clients, our work, and our co-workers than is healthy for us, or them. It can also cause us to react strongly, and at times without our conscious awareness, toward our clients or co-workers in ways that support division and conflict rather than unity and cooperation.

To be seen and heard, mirrored and accurately empathized with, are some of the strongest needs infants have during their development, needs that are highly associated with the infant's sense of physical and psychological survival. They're the basis for the development of the self and one of the strongest human motivations.

On the flip side, the fear of humiliation is one of our strongest counter-motivations. What we want or need the very most is what we're also most vulnerable to and dependent upon. We want to be acknowledged but are also afraid of being acknowledged. This is because the possibility of being noticed also brings the possibility of shame, of appearing bad or wrong.

The "Need-Desire" to Be Right

If being right is your goal,
you will find error in the world, and seek to correct it.
But do not expect peace of mind.
If peace of mind is your goal,
look for the errors in your beliefs and expectations.
Seek to change them, not the world.
And be always prepared to be wrong.

— Peter Russell, *Waking Up in Time*, page 95

Some care providers are burdened with a self-image that requires other people to respond to them in ways that they expect will make them feel right, important, and special. Such a burden can render opaque what would be transparent to someone less burdened. The need to be right can be experienced with a force and intensity the same as, or sometimes even greater than, the need to survive; many people are willing to be dead-right.

Eckhart Tolle in his recent book *Practicing the Power of Now,* observes that "Even such a seemingly trivial and 'normal' thing as the compulsive need to be right in an argument and make the other person wrong — defending the mental position with which you have identified — is due to the fear of death. If you identify with a mental position, then if you are wrong, your mind-based sense of

The need to be right can be experienced with a force and intensity the same as, or sometimes even greater than, the need to survive; many people are willing to be dead-right.

self is seriously threatened with annihilation. So you as the ego cannot be wrong."[8] When the desire to be seen and heard mutates into the compulsive need to be right, the force of that need-desire can be so strong that the experience of *being* wrong, as opposed to *doing* something wrong, is tantamount to emotional death. This accounts for why it's often so difficult to make conscious the unconscious dynamics behind some types of countertransference, particularly if you're experiencing a high degree of Compassion Fatigue, a state where you are the emotion, instead of experiencing the emotion.

The tendency to "sleepwalk" or lose your viewing point as the observer at the time you're experiencing intense countertransference reactions is increasingly intense and automatic the higher the degree of your Compassion Fatigue. During this state the rational, processing portion of the brain is progressively deactivated and the Limbic system, or emotional brain, is progressively hyper-activated. This process goes further and further as you experience more and more vicarious trauma.

Unless your awareness is grounded inside of your body and you can notice the tightening and restriction of the muscles in your neck, shoulders, stomach, and breathing, you'll experience a shift of perception from being present and observing to getting caught up inside the drama that is taking place in your mind, emotions, and body sensations. You're no longer watching your thoughts and emotions, you have identified with them. You experience that they *are* you.

Eckhart Tolle again writes that an "Intense presence is needed when certain situations trigger a reaction with a strong emotional charge, such as when your self-image is threatened, a challenge comes into your life that triggers fear, things 'go wrong,' or an emotional complex from the past is brought up. In those instances, the tendency is for you to become 'unconscious.'"[9] An "intense presence" constitutes being grounded in the body, emotionally centered, and consciously awake in the present moment.

"Unconsciousness" is the result of losing that presence when you feel your self-image being challenged; your body begins to freeze, your perception constricts, and your awareness narrows, locked into the need to be right.

The regular practice of conscious breathing and mindful movement in a harmonious flow of body, energy, and motion is one way to develop an intense presence that will result in greater enjoyment

and mastery of your profession as a caregiver. It will also begin to reverse and even prevent some of the physical and emotional conditions that often accompany our work as "the cost of caregiving." Being conscious of your self, of your body and mind working in conjunction, will prevent your observing part from being drawn in by a client's trauma and allow you to maintain that crucial balance between empathy and sympathy.

---

[8] Eckhart Tolle, *Practicing the Power of Now,* page 28

[9] *Ibid,* page 35

Chapter Two:

The Cost of Caregiving

Modern man has developed a social and economic structure and a sense of time urgency which subject him to more and greater stresses than have been experienced at any other time in human history, and the effect is often devastating.

— Kenneth R. Pelletier, *Mind as Healer, Mind as Slayer*, pages 3-4

The Cost of Stress

The cost of stress is staggering. According to the U.S. National Institute for Occupational Safety and Health, stress-related disorders are rapidly becoming the most prevalent reason for worker disability. Job stress is estimated to cost American industry 200 to 300 billion dollars annually, as assessed by absenteeism; diminished productivity; employee turnover; accidents; direct medical, legal, and insurance fees; workman's compensation awards; etc.

In 1992 the United Nations called job stress "The 20th Century Epidemic;" the World Health Organization called job stress a "World Wide Epidemic." It's estimated that 150 million dollars per year are lost by the U.S. due to stress-related absenteeism. Between the years 1980 and 1990 the number of stress disability claims made by California State Workers increased by more than 800 percent. Approximately 700 million dollars are spent each year to recruit replacement for executives with heart disease.

Chronic pain, hypertension, and headaches (three stress-related disorders) make up 54 percent of all job absenteeism. The American Institute of Stress reports that between 75 and 90 percent of visits to the doctor are related to stress, 60 to 80 percent of accidents on the job are related to stress, and 40 percent of staff turnover is due to stress at work. When considering these statistics, the term "epidemic" doesn't seem at all like an exaggeration.

Job Stress

The National Institute for Occupational Safety and Health (NIOSH) at www.cdc.gov/niosh/stresswk.html states "The nature of work is changing at whirlwind speed. Perhaps now more than ever before, job stress poses a threat to the health of workers, and in turn, to the health organizations." The website also explains that:

- 40 percent of workers report their job is "very or extremely stressful."

- One-fourth of employees view their jobs as the number one stressor in their lives.

- Three-fourths of employees believe the worker has more on the job stress than a generation ago.

- Problems at work are strongly associated with health complaints, even more than financial problems or family problems.

What is Job Stress?

NIOSH defines job stress as "The harmful physical and emotional responses that occur when the requirements of the job do not match the capabilities, resources, or needs of the worker." In fact NIOSH finds that job stress "can lead to poor health and even injury," and is now associated with the following conditions:

- **Cardiovascular Disease:** Many studies suggest that psychologically demanding jobs that allow employees little control over the work process increase the risk of cardiovascular disease.

- **Musculoskeletal Disorders:** On the basis of research by NIOSH and many other organizations, it's widely believed that job stress increases the risk for development of back and upper-extremity musculoskeletal disorders.

- **Psychological Disorders:** Several studies suggest that differences in rates of mental health problems, such as depression and burnout, for various occupations are due partly to differences in job stress levels.

- **Workplace Injury:** Although more study is needed, there's a growing concern that stressful working conditions interfere with safe work practices and set the stage for injuries at work.

- **Suicide, Cancer, Ulcers, and Impaired Immune Function:** Some studies suggest a relationship between stressful working conditions and these health problems. However, more research is needed before firm conclusions can be drawn.

Stress, Health, and Productivity

NIOSH recognizes that stress is counter-productive, citing studies that show a link between stressful work conditions and "increased absenteeism, tardiness, and intention by workers to quit, all of which have a negative effect on the bottom line…." The organization, at the web site www.cdc.gov/niosh/stresswk.html, also identified certain traits "associated with both healthy, low-stress work and high levels of productivity," such as

- Recognition of employees for good work performance.

- Opportunities for career development.

- An organizational culture that values the individual worker.

- Management actions that are consistent with organizational values.

According to NIOSH, St. Paul Fire and Marine Insurance Company conducted several studies on the effects of stress prevention programs in hospital settings. Program activities included employee and management education on job stress, changes in hospital policies and procedures to reduce organizational sources of stress, and establishment of employee assistance programs. In two studies it was reported that:

- The frequency of medication errors declined by 50 percent in one study at a 700-bed hospital that implemented stress prevention activities.

- There was a 70 percent reduction in malpractice claims in 22 hospitals that implemented stress prevention activities.

- There was no reduction in claims in a matched group of 22 hospitals that did not implement stress prevention activities.

It's pretty clear from all of these findings that job stress is more than just a nuisance to front line workers. Its impact is a ripple effect, affecting the health of employees, companies, and patients or clients.

Low Stress Tolerance

In addition to the already mentioned sources of stress at work, recent research points to another possible source of stress: low stress tolerance, a genetically inherited condition that affects the neural-chemical messengers in the brain. Some researchers believe that many of us were born with a tendency for certain neural-chemical messengers that handle emotional balance to stop functioning when they reach a certain level of stress. Low stress tolerance can cause a malfunction in the chemical messengers, such as Serotonin, which sets your body clock and allows you to sleep, Noradrenalin, which gives you energy, and Dopamine, which regulates pleasure and pain. When the production or transmission of these neural-chemicals is altered or interrupted the result can be chronic overstress and burnout. The concept that some of us may have a genetically inherited low stress tolerance would help to explain why at times we lose control at even slight provocations that seem out of proportion to what's happening at the time.

Care Provider Stress

The nature of caregiving itself may also produce a unique type of stress that's often under-identified and misunderstood; it's the stress that accompanies empathic engagement with patients who suffer from physical or emotional trauma. This care provider stress has been studied in professional and non-professional caregivers with some remarkable results. Numerous studies show a strong correlation between caregiving and depression, a sense of burden or overload, decreased immune function, and problems with concentration and memory. Also affected were coping strategies, interpersonal relationships, self-image, and self-esteem.

A number of professional journal articles associate the severity of certain symptoms and behaviors that traumatized patients often display with the level of burnout experienced by care providers. In one article entitled "Burnout and Compassion Fatigue

Among Hospice Caregivers," in *The American Journal of Hospice & Palliative Care,* the authors note that too frequently the reason behind the decision to leave or take a sabbatical from hospice work is that the staff member reached the limits of his or her capacity to care for or about patients and couldn't take it anymore. Another article, "Caregiver Burden and Psychological Distress in Partners of Veterans with Chronic Posttraumatic Stress Disorder," in *The Journal of Traumatic Stress,* claims that it's the severity of the symptoms of PTSD that are most associated with caregiver burden and distress. What both of these articles make clear is the correlation between patient trauma and its effects on those trying to help them.

The Role of Secondary Traumatic Stress

…[Secondary Traumatic Stress Disorder] is a syndrome of symptoms nearly identical to [Post Traumatic Stress Disorder] except that exposure to a traumatizing event experienced by one person becomes a traumatizing event of the second person.

– B. Hudnall Stamm, *Secondary Traumatic Stress,* page 11

Until recently, the role of trauma or traumatic stress on care provider stress has been largely overlooked. However, with more attention and research spent on patients with a diagnosis of Post Traumatic Stress Disorder (PTSD) in the last few years, there's increasing awareness of the effects secondary traumatic stress can have upon caregivers.

Secondary traumatic stress, also called vicarious trauma, can affect care providers in a manner similar to the way PTSD affects trauma survivors. Dr. B. Hudnall Stamm explains that "Vicarious traumatization is a process of change resulting from empathic engagement with trauma survivors. It can have an impact on the helper's sense of self, world view, spirituality, affect tolerance, interpersonal relationships, and imagery system of memory."[1]

Secondary traumatic stress differs from "ordinary stress," though, in much the same way Post Traumatic Stress Disorder is different than an anxiety disorder; the neural-chemical imprinting of traumatic stress often results in a type of implicit or "body" memory of the event that can be evoked without conscious awareness of, or "permission" from, the person experiencing it. According to *Listening to High Utilizers of Mental Health Services,* a 1999 state of Oregon report, secondary traumatic stress can have "profound and persistent alterations in physiologic reactivity and stress hormone secretion. A variety of triggers may come to precipitate extreme reactions, including both specific stimuli (related to the trauma itself) and neutral stimuli. To compensate for their chronic hyper-arousal, traumatized people may withdraw, shut down, or become emotionally numb and thus attempt to avoid the chronic noxious stimuli."[2]

The experience of traumatic stress results in the hyper-activation of certain neural-hormones that actually leave a "stamp" on the nervous system, causing the memory to be "frozen" in time. This non-declarative "body" memory can re-enact traumatic reactions *in the body* without warning and often without the ability to modulate the arousal. Furthermore, those caregivers who have experienced trauma in their own childhood may be much more vulnerable to absorbing and internalizing the emotions of their patients because of the fertile internal environment already seeded with implicit memory traces that can become activated in response to another person's traumatic stress reaction.

Horror Frozen in Memory

Dr. Goleman has coined the term "Horror Frozen in Memory" in his chapter "Trauma and Emotional Relearning" in *Emotional Intelligence,* and states "… the more brutal, shocking, and horrendous the events that trigger the amygdala hijacking, the more indelible the memory. The neural basis for these memories appears to be a sweeping alteration in the chemistry of the brain set in motion by a single instance of overwhelming terror. While the PTSD findings are typically based on the impact of a single

---

[1] B. Hudnall Stamm (ed), *Secondary Traumatic Stress,* page 52

[2] State of Oregon Report, *Listening to High Utilizers of Mental Health Services,* pages 12-13

episode, similar results can come from cruelties inflicted over a period of years, as is the case with children who are sexually, physically, or emotionally abused."[3] Dr. Goleman further explains "Some of the key changes are in the locus called catecholamines: adrenaline and noradrenaline. These neural-chemicals mobilize the body for an emergency; the same catecholamine surge stamps memories with special strength. In PTSD this system becomes hyperreactive, secreting extra-large doses of these brain chemicals in response to situations that hold little or no threat but are reminders of the original trauma…"[4]

For care providers who have experienced personal trauma in their lives, especially if they work with patients who are experiencing similar issues, the very process of providing care can render them much more vulnerable to absorbing and internalizing the "frozen in fear" Energy in *MOTION* of their patients and internalizing it as body memory.

Is the experience of trauma limited to those who have endured catastrophes such as September 11th? Dr. Goleman believes not. He writes "Fortunately, the catastrophic moments in which traumatic memories are emblazoned are rare during the course of life for most of us. But the same circuitry that can be seen so boldly imprinting traumatic memories is presumably at work in life's quieter moments, too. The more ordinary travails of childhood, such as being chronically ignored and deprived of attention or tenderness by one's parents, abandonment or loss, or social rejections may never reach the fever pitch of trauma, but they surely leave their imprint on the emotional brain, creating distortions — and tears and rages — in intimate relationships."[5]

Cumulative Traumatic Stress

Consistent with the experience of traumatic stress, secondary traumatic stress may be experienced in care providers either acutely, by co-experiencing a traumatic memory your patient is reliving, or cumulatively, over time, as the result of absorbing and internalizing the frozen energy of secondary traumatic stress. Even those care providers who have not experienced trauma directly in their lives can become vulnerable to secondary traumatic stress as a result of accumulating and storing the stress response as body memory.

Cumulative traumatic stress is insidious. It's the psychological equivalent of hypertension, "the silent killer." As our bodies unconsciously tighten, our muscles and breathing constrict in response to the repeated exposure of our patients' traumatic stress. Implicit memory traces are continually imprinted as body memory. The accumulation of this residual body memory is often described as burnout.

Burnout

Top Ten Signs You Are Suffering From Burnout

10. You're so tired you now answer the phone "Hell."

9. Your friends call to ask how you've been, and you immediately scream, "Get off my back!"

8. Your garbage can is your "in" box.

7. You wake up to discover your bed is on fire, but go back to sleep because you just don't care.

6. You have so much on your mind you've forgotten how to pee.

5. Visions of the upcoming weekend help you make it through Monday.

4. You sleep more at work than at home.

3. You leave for a party and instinctively bring your briefcase.

2. Your Day-Timer exploded a week ago.

1. You think about how relaxing it would be if you were in jail right now.

– Anonymous

---

[3] Daniel Goleman, *Emotional Intelligence,* page 203

[4] *Ibid,* page 205

[5] *Ibid,* page 213

As stress accumulates over a period of time through exposure to secondary trauma, especially for those of us who have a personal history of trauma or low stress tolerance and are without a specific strategy to identify and deal with it on an ongoing basis, cumulative stress can transform into burnout. Symptoms of burnout occur in four areas of a person's functioning:

Psychological-emotional symptoms of burnout include being critical of others, an apathetic attitude, depersonalizing patients, feelings of low personal accomplishment, frustration with others, boredom, depression, anxiety, hopelessness, poor concentration, irritability, and feelings of alienation and isolation.

Behavioral symptoms of burnout include spending less time with patients, exhibiting tardiness and absenteeism, committing medication errors, poor record keeping, abuse of alcohol or chemicals, impersonal or stereotyped communications, sarcasm, and cynicism.

Physical symptoms of burnout include a rapid pulse, insomnia, fatigue, reduced resistance to infection, weakness and dizziness, memory problems, weight changes, gastrointestinal complaints, frequent or lingering illnesses, hypertension, and head, back, or muscle aches.

Spiritual symptoms of burnout include doubt concerning one's value system or beliefs, drawing conclusions that a major change is necessary (such as divorce, a new job, or relocation), and becoming angry or bitter at God and withdrawing from fellowship.

Burnout and Control

Burnout, a problem in a wide variety of workplaces from emergency rooms to corporations, is compounded by mindlessness. Rigid mindsets, narrow perspectives, the trap of old categories, and an outcome orientation make burnout more likely. Conversely… changing contexts and mindsets, or focusing on process, can be energy-begetting.

– Ellen Langer, *Mindfulness*, pages 148-9

One of the major issues facing care providers today is the massive shift in the health care industry that in some contexts has resulted in increasing caseloads of chronically physically and mentally ill clients, increased paperwork and regulations, and a focus on outcome rather than process. Dr. Ellen Langer, the Harvard psychologist quoted above, notes that "Burnout sets in when two conditions prevail: Certainties start to characterize the workday, and demands of the job make workers lose a sense of control. If, in addition, an organization is characterized by rigid rules, problems that arise feel insurmountable because creative problem solving seems too risky."[6]

The question for care providers is "where do you have control and where don't you?" The section of the serenity prayer that goes "Grant me the serenity to accept the things I cannot change, the courage to change the things I can, and the wisdom to know the difference," appears particularly pertinent in regards to professional burnout.

The sense of losing control may be a result of the environment in which we work *and* our particular mindset about that environment. As care providers, we tend to be vulnerable to getting into a tug-of-war with "the administration" over issues neither we, nor they, can or will change. I still get flashbacks from the time I spent in the emergency room as a crisis worker. When I'm able to look back from a more detached point of view, I can see how my burnout was significantly affected by the feeling of powerlessness and lack of control over which patients, and how many of them, would come into the emergency room. As the years marched by, I became increasingly entrenched in my idea that I was merely a pawn for the administration, a front line soldier who was not at all important. I felt held hostage by my sense of (over-)responsibility for helping others on the one hand and my feeling used and devalued by the administration on the other.

The more need-desire I felt to be valued, important, and special, the more I felt used and abused. Despite the fact the administration did finally make some changes that included better coverage, steady days, and getting off weekend call, my perception had become locked into an adversarial relationship. I was also experiencing severe and persistent depression, a condition that nearly cost me my life.

---

[6] Ellen Langer, *Mindfullness,* page 149

Burned Out or Burned Up?

One of the things I remember about meeting my Sifu, or Qigong teacher, is the way he looked at and through me when we first met. I didn't know at that time that he was a Qigong master, a 10th degree black belt with the Chinese Martial Art Federation, a former bodyguard to the prime minister, or a member of the Singapore anti-terrorist task force. He was just Mr. Yong, a man my wife introduced to me during the time we lived in Singapore.

It was during a tea ceremony (he also teaches traditional Chinese Tea Ceremony) when Mr. Yong looked at me as I was describing my experience of burning out of the health care field and said "Your problem is not just a lack of Chi (energy), you have blocked the flow of Chi and this is causing you to burn up inside." What we typically label as burnout can be viewed as a condition that's characterized as much by the lack of movement of energy as a lack in energy. This lack burns us *up* as much as it burns us *out*. When we complain that we have no energy, it's often the case that our energy is blocked, not flowing or moving.

You can compare the flow of emotion to the flow of blood through your body. The blockage of blood through clogged arteries can affect your body in much the same way blockage of emotion can affect your sense of self: you experience fatigue, worry, anxiety, an overall feeling of weakness, and a fear of fragmenting or deteriorating. You're devoid of energy, flexibility, and enthusiasm. To take the analogy a step further, we can even imagine the hardened, crusted cholesterol that restricts the flow of life-giving blood/energy, as those rigid, inflexible, belief systems that encrust and restrict the flow of emotion.

The very action of being tense is to tighten your muscles and restrict your breathing in preparation for fight, flight, or freeze. Because the source of your stress is often hidden from your conscious awareness, you can become chronically tense to where you don't even notice it. The body's reaction is similar to your car if you were to hold one foot on the gas and one on the break every time you put it into gear.

Rigid mindsets, narrow perspectives, the trap of old categories, and an outcome orientation make burnout more likely.

— Ellen Langer, *Mindfulness,* pages 148-9

Depression

Some Statistics from the National Depressive and Manic Depressive Association:

1. Depression affects nearly 10 percent of adult Americans.

2. Nearly twice as many women as men get depressed.

3. Only one in 10 Americans receives adequate treatment for depression.

4. Major depression is the number one cause of disability.

5. Clinical depression costs 53 billion dollars annually.

6. Depression affects 340 million people in the world each year.

7. Depression accounts for 10 percent of productive years lost.

8. Half of all cases of depression go unrecognized.

9. About 10 to 15 percent of depressed people complete suicide.

10. The World Health Organization predicts that by 2020 depression will be the greatest burden of ill health and the second cause of death and disability in the developing world.

Compassion Fatigue and Depression

If stress and burnout are like the emotional cholesterol that can clog and harden our arteries, then depression *is* like a heart attack. In many ways, depression is an attack on the heart, often with devastating results.

Depression is one of the most often co-morbid diagnoses made with PTSD. It's natural to consider it as a consequence of traumas many care providers who suffer from Compassion Fatigue have experienced earlier in life. Candace Pert Ph.D., author of *Molecules of Emotion,* writes that "recently, researchers at the National Institutes of Health have found a link between depression and traumas experienced in early childhood. Studies have shown that abused, neglected, or otherwise unnurtured infants and children are more likely to be depressed as adults."[7] It's no wonder that so many of us in the caregiving field have, are, or will experience a major depressive episode at some point in our career, seeing as we are likely either to have experienced trauma personally or absorbed it from our patients.

There are many different forms of and individual differences in our own personal experiences of depression. I've had the opportunity to share my individual account of depression with many colleagues, seminar participants, and patients and have found some themes that parallel my own personal experience of depression.

The Personal Experience of Depression

The personal experience of depression, the personal experience of any mental illness, is sometimes difficult to describe; more often it's difficult to understand, especially for those who haven't known it themselves. There's a constant, ongoing adjustment process between people with severe and persistent mental illness and those who care about us. I can remember how my friends and family were lost and bewildered when I tried to describe my helpless descent into that dark, foreboding, bottomless pit of emotional agony that has the power to stop time, movement, and energy. Until you have felt the talons of that Dragon it's very difficult to understand its power.

Depression, particularly acute depression, is a lesson in humility. We like to think that we're in complete control of our thoughts, feelings, and actions. This isn't always the case. The experience of acute depression will undermine any idea you may have had that you're in total, or at times *any,* control of your thoughts and feelings. The sense of utter helplessness in not being able to "snap out of it" as your very sense of life drains away often causes us to insult

---

[7] Candace Pert, *Molecules of Emotion,* page 269

and emotionally batter ourselves on top of the depression. But you can't bring yourself up by knocking yourself down.

Depression often begins with me slowly, silently, with a stealth and ease that characterizes its dark intentions. Many people won't recognize the very beginning of their depression until they become transparent enough with themselves to see the true intent of their thoughts, feelings, and actions when they first began to form. As difficult as it is for us to look at, our depressions often start as the result of a specific, repeated intent to be depressed. The part of ourselves that repeats this intent is most often split off from our central awareness and we only wake up to it when we form and hold the conscious intent to do so. This disowned or dissociated part is hyper-vigilant to environmental cues that are perceived as evidence or affirmations that you really are to blame, that you truly are basically flawed, defected, and do indeed deserve to be hurt and punished.

As the experience of depression progresses, chronic withdrawal leaves you with the feeling/sense of being numb and unreal; your body feels thick, lethargic, without life or energy, and you can feel trapped inside, isolated and alone. You find your awareness plummeting into depths of pain and darkness that seem to have no bottom. I would often experience a sense of sinking behind my face as though there were three feet of skin between me and the world. As my awareness retreated I could actually feel my sense of self being pulled apart, fragmenting, like I was being literally torn into pieces.

As the depression continued I would begin to lose perspective. There was no longer an observing "me" watching the pain. I was the pain. Thoughts, images, and scenarios of suicide began to parade across my consciousness. They came louder and harder. And at some point there was always a snap. The "snap" is a sudden shift of perception, an emotional hijacking. Thoughts and ideas that were once abhorrent now appeared to make perfectly good sense. The idea of suicide no longer seemed strange or out of place. In fact it seemed natural, even comforting.

This is when depression is the most dangerous. There's often a sense of inner resolve that to other people appears to be an improvement. You seem less dark and heavy and may even have energy and be able to joke about things. There's no real depth to these feelings, though, because your entire perception has been hijacked by a brain gone mad, a brain that believes the only solution is its own destruction. Acute depression may require immediate action from mental health professionals who are trained to intervene in emergency situations and are usually accessed through the local county or state mental health system. With awareness, however, and preventative measures, there's rarely a good reason for depression to progress this far.

Numerous studies have shown, over and over again, the immediate, direct, and positive impact physical exercise has on relieving and preventing depression. The problem with this method is that, when you're depressed, exercise is the *last* thing on your mind; you can't begin to imagine yourself running or riding a stationary bike or going to an aerobics class. Depression generates a general antipathy toward moving, and for that reason I developed a strain-free, quick exercise based on Qigong that sufferers could undertake easily and immediately — FlowMotion™.

The mindful movement of FlowMotion™ is probably quite different than most exercises you've done in the past; you don't need a health club, any machines, or special equipment; you're not going to exercise yourself into a sweat for 60 minutes to the pounding beat of a dance video; and you're not going to want to distract your attention from the body experience of the exercise by watching television. FlowMotion™ is a slow, fluid, continuous movement that's done in harmony with your breath for a total of 5 to 10 minutes. All the movement is done in a standing position and can be done virtually anywhere. Most importantly, FlowMotion™ is done for the enjoyment of the movement and energy, the integration of body and mind.

Chapter Three:

Parallel Process

All hearts exchange information with other hearts and brains. Cardiac energy patterns have dynamic interactive effects. When one heart sends energy to another, that energy becomes a part of the receiving heart's memory. When the receiving heart becomes a sending heart, the energy it sends is no longer just its own.

— Paul Pearsall, *The Heart's Code*, page164

Introduction

Fascinating insights have started emerging from recent investigations into the non-local energy dynamics of the heart and the circulation of emotion throughout the entire body, insights that begin to point toward the inescapable realization that we're all very, very connected to each other.

In *The Heart's Code* Dr. Paul Pearsall's research indicates that the heart may be more than just the most efficient pump ever designed; this particular organ may also be connected with *Energy* in *MOTION* in a way that's central to understanding parallel process. He poses the question of whether it's "possible that a subtle form of energy [called] life or 'L' energy and which others refer to as a 'healing' or 'X' force carries information and that, just as Albert Einstein showed us that energy and matter are interchangeable, information and energy are also synonymous?"[1]

Energy in MOTION: The Fifth Force

The "fifth force," or "L" energy as described by Dr. Pearsall, draws upon the fields of sub-atomic physics and quantum mechanics to describe some of its unique characteristics, such as non-locality, which allows energy and information to be in more than one person, one heart at a time. Dr. Persall explains that "L" energy travels faster than the speed of light. At more than 186,000 miles per second, it radiates out everywhere within and from you, accounting for the 'nonlocal' effects of occurrences such as telepathy, remote healing, and the power of intercessory prayer."[2]

I often ask seminar participants if any of them has ever had a personal experience of "knowing" through direct intuition about a physical/emotional/medical trauma involving someone emotionally close but living at a distance. Invariably, 30 to 40 percent of them will raise their hands. When asked if any of them has personally experienced distance healing 10 to 15 percent raise their hands. As

much as these concepts may butt against our traditional views of medicine, they've been gaining acceptance. How could they be possible if we're not somehow directly, "non-locally" connected with others?

Distance healing and other forms of complementary medicine are now being examined in some controlled studies at the Duke Center for Integrative Medicine. What's becoming clear is that our traditional paradigm of causality must undergo a transformation to explain in our mind what we already know in our hearts. It's not infrequent for several participants to approach me after the workshop to talk about personal experiences of healing that were in direct contradiction to our current medical paradigm. They generally feel embarrassed to share with their professional colleagues for fear of being judged as "new age."

It's a shame that, despite the Duke University Center's findings that 40 percent of Americans already regularly use alternative medicine (costing them more than 30 billion dollars of their own money) and that there are more visits annually to alternative providers than to primary care physicians, many of us in the healthcare profession are hesitant to even consider these non-traditional, "unscientific" explanations for healing and feel embarrassed to admit we have had a personal experience ourselves.

'L' energy is nonlocal or free of the limits of space and time as we know them. It is everywhere at the same time, meaning that tuning in to this energy is not as much a matter of 'sending' or 'receiving' as 'connecting.'

— Paul Persall, *The Heart's Code,* page 54

Because care providers, particularly those who work with trauma patients, are almost universally highly empathic, we "connect" with our patients' *Energy* in *MOTION* even when we're not physically with them, sometimes even when we're not consciously thinking about them. The ability to have a direct connection and perception of another person's energy is one of the most difficult things for us to accept, even though we know it in our bones. I think some

---

[1] Paul Persall, *The Heart's Code,* page 5

[2] *Ibid,* page 53

of our difficulty with this concept has its roots in what we like to believe in our culture is "individuality" and "independence."

One of the more tragic and dangerous misconceptions that's alive and growing in the United States today is the mistake of thinking of individualism and independence as isolation and disconnection. It's very uncomfortable for many of us in contemporary society to imagine just how interdependent all human beings are. In reality, we can think of ourselves like trees: above the ground of consciousness we appear very separate, yet beneath the apparent illusion of separation we are very connected to each other, through the earth and through our roots.

The heart is uniquely composed of 'L' energy and communicates and conveys it in its own form but is also 'piggybacked' on the electromagnetic field (EMF) created by the heart.

— Paul Persall, *The Heart's Code,* page 55

The understanding that the heart may actually be the center for a type of emotional energy and intelligence isn't a recent innovation. For centuries Indian and Chinese traditions have viewed the heart as a powerful vortex of energy and information. Just recently, though, some new technology has begun to identify and describe the energy, in scientific terms, that's transmitted by the heart. Dr. Pearsall reports that "The heart's EMF [electromagnetic field] is five thousand times more powerful than the electromagnetic field created by the brain and, in addition to its immense power, has subtle, nonlocal effects that travel within these forms of energy. Superconducting quantum interference devices, magnetocardiograms, and magnetoencepholograms that measure magnetic fields outside the body show that the heart generates over fifty thousand femtoteslas (a measure of EMF) compared to less than ten femtoteslas recorded from the brain."[3]

The ego is a legend in its own mind because of its self-anointed self-importance. Despite the fact that the heart is more powerful than the brain and has influence over the body and mind in ways the ego can't imagine, the ego continues to perceive itself as the master of the brain and as an isolated object that must control other

---

[3] *Ibid,* page 55

'L' energy is nonlocal or free of the limits of space and time as we know them. It is everywhere at the same time.

— Paul Persall, *The Heart's Code,* page 54

egos. Long ago Fritz Perls, the founder of Gestalt, advised "Lose your mind and come to your senses!" I don't think Perls really advocated completely letting go of all mental processes, but he has a great point in that we must learn to trust our hearts as well as our heads.

'L' energy fills all of space in the form of bundles of vibrating energy that can manifest themselves as either particles or waves that contain the information transmitted within, and to, all persons and things.

— Paul Persall, *The Heart's Code*, page 55

It's interesting to consider the idea that all of what we visually comprehend as empty space may actually be filled with bundles of vibrating energy and information that can be felt and recognized by an empathic, receiving heart. It might also be interesting to consider how the variations in frequency, intensity, or pulsation of this energy might affect us, physically and emotionally.

Two of the oldest established forms of medicine, Chinese and Japanese medicine, are based on subtle energy, which is called 'Qi' or 'Chi' in China and 'Ki' in Japan.

— Paul Persall, *The Heart's Code*, page 58

The idea that "L" energy and Qi energy are similar or the same in function helps explain the personal experiences in emotional healing I've had through Qigong, or "the art of cultivating Qi."

When I first moved to Singapore I was just divorced from an unhappy marriage and experienced a traumatic end to my career with a large HMO as a crisis intervention specialist. I was in therapy for Post Traumatic Stress Syndrome and clinical depression and taking Prozac. I was recently re-married to my current wife, a Singapore citizen. It was in this context I learned Qigong.

To practice Qigong and experience the unfreezing of old, stagnant, hardened-in-the-body emotion into the fluid, flowing, dancing energy of Qi is to have the physical, emotional, and mental experience of flow. My intellectual ideas about energy were quickly replaced with the real, in-the-body experience of living, flowing energy. After six months of Qigong I threw away my prescription for Prozac.

Learning and practicing Qigong was possibly the most direct, physical, real experience of Energy in *MOTION* I could have. There's no room for intellectual doubt. As your awareness circulates with breath and energy both inside and outside your body simultaneously you realize that you're not at all an isolated ego trapped in a body. Qigong is a direct experience of parallel process, the vibrating energy that's both here and there, inside and outside, me and you simultaneously. It dissolves the illusion that a separate, entitled, although fragile, "need to be right" ego, resides at the center of our being and awareness. In my case, the practice of Qigong opened my heart as much as my eyes to the subtle flow of energy, information, and awareness that connects more than it separates, that includes more than it excludes and nourishes the sense of being good enough.

Secondary Traumatic Stress — the Body of Evidence

Traumatic symptoms are not caused by the triggering event itself. They stem from the frozen residue of energy that has not been resolved and discharged; this residue remains trapped in the nervous system where it can wreak havoc on our bodies and spirits. The long-term, alarming, debilitating, and often bizarre symptoms of PTSD develop when we cannot complete the process of moving in, through and out of the immobility or freezing state.

— Peter Levine, *Waking the Tiger: Healing Trauma*, page 19

As Dr. Levine so eloquently explains, the symptoms of PTSD and Compassion Fatigue are the result of the frozen residue of energy that hasn't been resolved or discharged from your body where it can remain trapped in the nervous system. The body reaction to this energy is to tighten and freeze, to constrict muscles and restrict breath.

The Body Keeps the Score

The idea that traumatic memories can be recorded in the body as implicit memory has begun to gain wide acceptance in the traumatic stress therapy community. It helps explain the intensity of body sensations that care providers suffering from Compassion Fatigue often experience.

To reiterate what was explained before, through empathic engagement care providers repeatedly open their hearts to the frozen emotional energy of their traumatized patients that may also activate the care provider's dormant "residue" of personal trauma. The re-exposure to this traumatic stress automatically initiates a freeze response in the care provider similar to what the patient is experiencing. The freeze response triggers powerful hormones that cause the body to tense, particularly in the neck and shoulders, and restrict breathing. The care provider is also likely to experience the "mental" experience of dissociation. The physical freeze response is intimately connected with the experience of mental-dissociation and this physical-freezing/mental-dissociation can occur for years after a traumatic event.

Is it also possible to consider the process of dissociation to occur along a continuum, from the jarring experience of being shocked "out of your body," at one extreme end, and chronic worry, obsessive mental rumination, and distraction on the other? How about the physical freezing response? Wouldn't there also be a continuum from the shock/numbing/statue state on one end and the tight/jittery/fatigued state on the other?

Because we're so chronically frozen and rarely consciously experience an alternate state of physical, emotional, and mental flow, we've come to mistake this habitual tightness, fatigue, and mental fragmentation as "normal." The part of you that experiences this state as the regular, everyday way of life is your ego awareness, not your body/mind or natural awareness. Once you begin to transfer your awareness from your head/ego to your heart-body/Natural Self, an entirely different set of perceptions and experiences begin to emerge. You begin to notice how alive your body really is and you start to enjoy being able to fully live inside of it. You begin to trust the intuitive nudges of your Natural Self.

Emotions for Every Body

Mind doesn't dominate body, it becomes the body — body and mind are one. I see the process of communication we have demonstrated, the flow of information throughout the whole organism, as evidence that the body is the actual outward manifestation, in physical space, of the mind.

— Candace Pert, *Molecules of Emotion*, page 187

Candace Pert Ph.D. is a Research Professor at the Department of Physiology and Biophysics at Georgetown University. She was one of the researchers who discovered what we now call "endorphins," the body's own natural opiate-like substances that, as every athlete knows, are responsible for the "runner's high." In her book *Molecules of Emotion* Dr. Pert disputes the traditional paradigm that emotions are the result of electrical signals that are stimulated in various parts of the brain. Her research and discoveries show that emotions are the result of various neural-hormones that bond with certain receptor sites on cells located all over the brain *and body*. She explains that "Emotional states or moods are produced by the various neuropeptide ligands, and what we experience as an emotion or a feeling is also a mechanism for activating a particular neuronal circuit — simultaneously throughout the brain and body — which generates a behavior involving the whole creature, with all the necessary physiological changes that behavior requires."[4]

The concept that traumatic stress is both a type of non-local energy that can be empathically sensed and "connected" to, heart to heart, as well as a "mechanism for activating a particular neuronal circuit simultaneously throughout the brain and body" can help explain intellectually what many care providers know intuitively: we're much more connected to the emotional stress and trauma some of our patients experience than we would like to think.

---

[4] Candace Pert, *Molecules of Emotion*, page 145

The Self as a Central Organizing Function

At present, trauma experts consider pathology of the self to be the main adverse phenomenon in trauma patients. Inspired by Kohut's self psychology and psychoanalytical object relations theory, Ulman and Brothers (1988) and Mcann and Perlman (1990) postulate a shattering of the self in trauma survivors. A division into so-called "good" and "bad" self-representations is the result. Therefore, the focus of treatment is the integration of the self and thereby restoration of the sense of self-coherence in trauma survivors.

— Bessel Van der Kolk, *Traumatic Stress,* page 371

Another way in which parallel process affects care providers is how we attend to ourselves, others, and our environment, basically how we process information. Bessel Van der Kolk, M.D., has researched and written extensively on how the mental/emotional/physical experience of trauma can fragment the survivor's basic sense of self, disrupting the sense of self-continuity and coherency. This fragmentation in a person's self-structure will disturb and disrupt the ability to perceive him- or herself, others, and the environment in a whole or integrated fashion. Survivors are prone to perceptual and emotional distortions.

What is the Self?

The concept of "self" has been utilized in many different psychological theories and formulations that can vary greatly, and its definitions range from another term for ego to a semi-mystical description of the soul. Heinz Kohut was a psychoanalyst who wrote extensively about the self and utilized the term precisely and specifically to describe the psychological development of an infant from the stage of primary narcissism to self-consolidation and cohesion. He defines the nuclear self in *The Restoration of the Self* as "The basis for our sense of being an independent center of initiative and perception, integrated with our most central ambitions and ideals

At present, trauma experts consider pathology of the self to be the main adverse phenomenon in trauma patients.

— Bessel Van der Kolk,
Traumatic Stress, page 371

and with our experience that our body and mind form a unit in space and a continuum in time."[5]

In Kohut's Self-Psychology, the nuclear self is the central organizing function of the individual that provides a person with the mind/body sense of continuity in time and space. It's more basic than self-image or self-esteem. It's the experience of even having a coherent sense of being, of experiencing psychological "substance."

Development of the Self

Kohut traces the development of the self back to a stage of primary narcissism where there is only minimal recognition of another. It's through "empathic mirroring" that the developing child begins to perceive the presence of others or "objects," as seen through the need-satisfying eyes of the child. In early childhood, others are first perceived by the child emotionally as "need-satisfying self-objects." In this sense, every perception of another person or "object" has a component of the self imbedded in it as well so that other people are actually experienced emotionally as extensions of the self. This is a central concept in understanding Compassion Fatigue. The more fragmented your sense of self, the more "in pieces" you feel emotionally, the greater your tendency to experience other people, particularly those you're emotionally frustrated with, as self-extended "objects." This situation interferes with attempts to satisfy your own urgent need-desires.

What we're often unaware of is the fact that the part of the "other," or object, that we're most frightened by or frustrated and angry with is actually a part of our own devalued selves that we've split off, disowned, and projected onto the "object screen" of the other person. The more you split and disown parts of your personality (because you experience them as bad or intolerable), the more you must compensate by creating and identifying with an inflated sense of self-entitlement to counter-balance the devalued and disowned self. The more you identify with self-aggrandizing images, roles, and expectations that are created and sustained primarily to counter-balance the secret, devalued, and disowned emotions and images within you, the greater the split and disharmony within your personality structure and the "weaker" and less coherent you

feel. That's the tragic flaw to this type of ego-logic, the greater you become the less you are.

Self-Coherence and Continuity

Each succeeding phase in human development demands a (re)establishment of psychic coherence and continuity. Self-coherence and self-continuity are closely related concepts. They are essential to feeling that one is a whole person. Self-coherence refers to integration in the here and now, while self-continuity refers to the feeling of integrity in retrospect, over the entire life-span.

— Bessel Van der Kolk, *Traumatic Stress*, page 370

Self-coherence and continuity are essential to feeling like a "whole person," a state that begins to break down and fragment under the barrage of secondary traumatic stress. Feeling like a whole person is a physical, emotional, and mental state of integration in which your awareness feels comfortable residing in the here and now, physical/emotional reality of your body-mind. It's characterized by a deep, in the bones sense of "good-enoughness." "Good-enoughness" is the result of accepting yourself as you are, as you remember yourself in the past and how you imagine yourself to be in the future. It's feeling coherent enough to have a realistic and compassionate sense of yourself and others; you're neither lost in adulation nor disgusted in disbelief. You sense yourself as an emotional center of gravity, you feel solidly inside your body and you're in tune with your heart and the emotions of others.

Under the barrage of traumatic energy that care providers routinely absorb and internalize, our sense of self-coherence and continuity can begin to fragment, to come undone. Rather than experiencing yourself and others in whole images, sensations, and emotions integrated with a sense of meaning, you feel as though you're "going to pieces," or "coming apart at the seams." Your world becomes increasingly chaotic and dangerous as people and events seem to turn against you.

---

[5] Heinz Kohut, *Restoration of the Self,* page 177

Dissociation and Self-Fragmentation

In addition to the emotional splitting that Compassion Fatigue or secondary traumatic stress can precipitate, the defense mechanism of dissociation itself is a type of perceptual splitting. The very act of dissociating is to split one aspect of the experience apart from another and to hold them separate. This form of perceptual splitting not only results in distortions and disturbances in the way in which information is processed, it also forms fissures in the self-structure, weakening, enfeebling, even fracturing and fragmenting the self.

Recent research suggests that dissociation can be a now *and* later event, happening immediately, some time down the road, or in some combination of those two time frames. In chronic dissociation the dissociated state itself becomes normative and the experience of self-cohesion and continuity is often fleeting and not recognized when it does occur. Acute or sudden dissociation is often accompanied by feelings of unreality, depersonalization, "out of body" experiences, and partial or total loss of explicit memory. In each case, chronic or acute dissociation, self-cohesion, and continuity are compromised. There's greater emotional and behavioral instability, perception and cognition are distorted, and significant disturbances manifest that disrupt the mind's ability to tell which information is processed. As one social worker who works exclusively with sexual abuse victims told me, "It's as though you were seeing your life every day as if you were looking into a mirror that's been broken into a hundred pieces; a fragmented reflection is all you see. You don't even realize it's the mirror that's broken."

Disturbances in Information Processing

When suffering from Compassion Fatigue, when we've absorbed and internalized the trauma of our patients, we can actually begin to mirror some of the same information processing disturbances as our patients that can distort the way in which we perceive ourselves, our relationships with patients, our co-workers, and our work. In his work with trauma survivors who suffer from PTSD, Dr. Van der Kolk, in *Traumatic Stress,* identifies "six critical issues that affect how people with PTSD process information."[6] These disturbances also parallel similar challenges care providers with Compassion Fatigue struggle with as well.

(1) They experience persistent intrusions of memories related to the trauma, which interfere with attending to other incoming information…[7]

Persistent intrusions need not only manifest as flashbacks and visual memories. Many intrusions may be experienced as intense emotional instability, sudden shifts in perception and behavior, body sensations, obsessive thoughts, or partial images. They can also manifest over time in the structure of your personality (as particular traits), in your relationships with others, and even as themes that weave themselves throughout your life. Van der Kolk explains that "These intrusions of traumatic memories can take many different shapes: flashbacks; intense emotions, such as panic or rage; somatic sensations; nightmares; interpersonal reenactments; character styles; and pervasive life themes."[8] Constant exposure to experiencing the traumatic stress of our patients, particularly if we're trauma survivors ourselves, can precipitate intrusions from our own pasts. For care providers who have repeated contact with trauma survivors, persistent intrusions can become an ordinary occurrence, so much so that we come to accept this condition as "normal."

I don't think anyone alive today is a stranger to persistent intrusions on the consciousness. They've become commonplace in

---

[6] Bessel Van der Kolk, *Traumatic Stress,* page 9

[7] *Ibid,* page 9

[8] *Ibid,* page 9

our current society, so woven into the fabric of daily life that our attention is literally hijacked every minute by the computer, the internet, the television, the radio, billboards, magazines, and every form of advertisement that's designed specifically to take and hold our attention. In a very real sense the ongoing and oppressing focus on terror in every form of media, as well as the constant day-to-day pressure of emotional survival, can create a self-sustaining feedback circuit that can kindle our emotions until we experience spontaneous emotional combustion.

Past traumas are often compartmentalized and dissociated from the central personality. Even having no memory of trauma in your own life does not necessarily mean you didn't experience something. Empathic connection to another person's trauma can suddenly and forcefully open previously locked perceptual and emotional compartments. We can become easily overwhelmed and then shut down; we withdraw and often develop depression. Van der Kolk explains "One of the serious complications that interferes with healing is that one particular event can activate another, long-forgotten memory of previous traumas, and create a 'domino effect.' A person who was not previously bothered by intrusive and distressing memories may, after exposure to yet another event, develop such memories of earlier experiences."[9]

Because we may sometimes work in environments that don't acknowledge the intensity of this work, the emotional wear and tear is ignored and intensifies. Rather than hearing the internal scream of your heart as your body goes into another involuntary freezing response, you continue to push yourself to meet the demands of our frenzied, traumatized society. As one care provider at a recent seminar stated "I've been a therapist for years without a single memory of having been traumatized as a child. It wasn't until I started working with sexual abuse perpetrators mandated by the court for counseling that I began to have intense stomach and bowel problems and was diagnosed with colitis. For weeks I had intense, intrusive pain. I also began to have sudden and intense rage attacks usually after working with a particular client. After about six months I developed depression. I could not sleep even though I was physically and emotionally exhausted all the time. I was getting further and further behind on my chart work. Relationships at home with my partner also began to deteriorate and we were just about ready to split when I finally got into therapy and started exercising. The long and short of it is, working with sexual abuse

perpetrators, particularly this one client, precipitated very early memories of having been sexually abused as a young girl."

(2)[T]hey sometimes compulsively expose themselves to situations reminiscent of the trauma…[10]

In my seminar "How to Transform Compassion Fatigue," care providers who work with physical abuse survivors will sometimes ask in disbelief "Why does someone who has been brutally attacked and battered by their partner get out of one abusive relationship, go out and find another person who will abuse them like their first partner?"

Van der Kolk explains that "One set of behaviors that is not mentioned in the diagnostic criteria for PTSD is the compulsive re-exposure of some traumatized individuals to situations reminiscent of the trauma…In this reenactment of the trauma, an individual may play the role of either victimizer or victim."[11] As previously mentioned, upwards of 75 to 90 percent of the participants in my seminars identify themselves as trauma survivors. Is it really any wonder we're drawn, at times compulsively driven, to work with survivors who are often experiencing the very same kind of trauma we experienced in our own lives?

While I believe the majority of us are care providers because we have great concern for others and wouldn't intentionally harm another person, compulsive re-exposure to trauma may make us more vulnerable to causing unintentional harm. Counter-transference issues may arise that cause us to feel and act in ways that are perceived by patients and coworkers as unsafe or toxic and we may be completely unaware of it. We may re-construct and re-enact our personal trauma in the arena of our professions.

Re-victimization can manifest itself in a number of different ways. We often experience being the victim of emotional or physical abuse in our primary relationship with our partners and significant others. We can also become a victim of "the system" in which we work. In each case we find that we're compulsively drawn to people, relationships, and situations that will have a high probability of

---

[9] *Ibid,* page 340

[10] *Ibid,* page 9

[11] *Ibid,* page 10

re-exposing us to the trauma that's reminiscent of our past personal trauma. It can precipitate self-destructive behavior, a set of traits that are legendary among care providers. We destroy ourselves in a host of ways including agreeing to unreasonable work schedules, demands, and expectations. There's also the continual barrage of self-deprecating thoughts and feelings and compulsive behaviors including overeating and abusing alcohol and drugs. Depression and suicidal thoughts, feelings, and behaviors are not uncommon among care providers. I often joke with fellow professionals that we probably keep the pharmaceutical industry in the black.

I recently ran into a nurse on one of the medical units at an older established hospital I often visit when performing mental health investigations in Oregon. I remembered her as being a psychiatric nurse at one of the newer HMO hospitals in the valley that had a reputation for burning out nurses. She looked much more relaxed than I had seen her at the other hospital. Over lunch she explained the change. She told me "I finally had to get out of psych nursing, out of that hospital and off that unit or I was going to end up in that unit! I could never understand why I kept going back there even though I hated the charge nurse, always pulled the weekend, and always, always got the toughest patients until I finally quit and got into counseling. It was the best thing I could have done." This particular nurse, after going through counseling, discovered her own tendencies toward re-traumatization and took the positive step of finding a less traumatic work place.

(3) [T]hey actively attempt to avoid specific triggers of trauma-related emotions, and experience a generalized numbing of responsiveness…[12]

In a trauma survivor's life, a considerable percentage of our most valuable natural resources, our time, energy, attention, and intention, can be spent avoiding internal and external triggers that can precipitate the distressing re-experiencing of traumatic emotions. Trauma-related emotions are most often intense fear, panic, rage, and depression. These emotions are so threatening to self-cohesion and consolidation they're usually disowned and dissociated. Triggers can be as innocuous as an image, memory, sound, smell, or even body sensation that will suddenly and forcefully stimulate a trauma-related emotion.

One of the problems care providers have is the continual re-exposure to a variety of internal and external triggers in the course of seeing patients who are experiencing trauma. Avoiding re-exposure

to these triggers is very difficult to do externally during the course of a day. We often find other forms of avoidance. Van der Kolk writes, "Avoidance may take many different forms, such as keeping away from reminders, ingesting drugs or alcohol in order to numb awareness of distressing emotional states, or utilizing dissociation to keep unpleasant experience from conscious awareness."[13] Triggers don't just emanate from patients, either. We may be constantly re-exposed to trauma through our day-to-day interactions with our co-workers as well. The more sensitive and vulnerable we are to the emotions, situations, and behaviors of both patients and co-workers, the more we'll feel the need to avoid making empathic contact with them or anyone else around us.

Avoidance can take the form of minimizing both the quality and quantity of contact we have with others. We may find ourselves constantly late for work, looking for ways to avoid certain patients or coworkers, or shutting down emotionally when we do have contact. We can find ourselves becoming increasingly numb physically, emotionally withdrawn, and socially isolated. Van der Kolk explains that "many people with PTSD not only actively avoid emotional arousal, but experience a progressive decline and withdrawal, in which any stimulation (whether it is potentially pleasurable or aversive) provokes further detachment. To feel nothing seems to be better than feeling irritable and upset."[14] Numbing is an actual physical experience that's often controlled by physical tension and the way we breathe. The best way to numb yourself physically is to take short, shallow, restricted breaths while tensing the muscles that connect your shoulders and neck. This will restrict both oxygen and blood supply to the rest of your body, creating the sensation of numbing.

Take a moment right now and focus your attention on the muscles that connect your shoulders to your neck. How do they feel? Can you feel them? Are they numb? Is there tension, tightness, pain, or numbness? Have you been chronically tensing these muscles without noticing it?

Allow yourself to consciously tighten these muscles by squeezing and moving them, forwards, up, and then back as you breathe in.

---

[12] *Ibid*, page 9

[13] *Ibid*, page 12

[14] *Ibid*, page 12

Really squeeze them as you rotate your shoulders and draw in a breath from your diaphragm.

When you've breathed in a full breath and have rotated your shoulders, tightly hold your muscles and your breath for just a couple of seconds. Then allow your shoulders to drop down and forward as you allow your breath to discharge with a "whoosh!"

What happens? Can you begin to feel a little sensation with the circulation? Try the exercise again and visualize that you're loosening, thawing and discharging old, blocked, frozen energy that has accumulated from years of tension. Each time your attention is able to enter into the muscle itself, you actually "feed" the muscles and nerves with energy, as well as oxygenated blood.

Focus on your breath. How much effort is required to take in a full breath from your diaphragm? How frozen are the muscles of your belly and abdomen? One of the simple reasons you don't have much energy at the end of the day is because you restrict and hold in your energy by restricting and holding in your breath. When you begin to consciously relax and breathe fully you may begin to experience more body sensations, as well as the soothing of chronic muscle aches.

(4) [T]hey lose the ability to modulate their physiological responses to stress in general, which leads to a decreased capacity to utilize bodily signals as guides for action…[15]

Losing the ability to modulate physiological responses to stress means you lose your ability to soothe and calm yourself down when you get stressed out. This is perhaps one of the most familiar symptoms of Compassion Fatigue that nearly every care provider has experienced, the tendency to just "lose it," at times in response to a situation that was not that important. For some of us it's overwhelming rage, for others it's fragmenting anxiety or the implosion of depression. The common denominator is the experience of utter helplessness to stop or even slow down the progression of emotions. Van der Kolk writes "People with PTSD tend to move immediately from stimulus to response without often realizing what makes them so upset. They tend to experience intense negative emotions (fear, anxiety, anger, and panic) in response to even minor stimuli: as a result, they either overreact and threaten others, or shut down and freeze."[16]

When the Limbic system is chronically aroused, stimulating the production of adrenaline, the prefrontal cortex, the part of the brain that regulates behavior, can become less activated. As care providers are continually exposed and re-exposed, day in and day out, to the traumatic stress of their patients, their organization, the healthcare industry, and even the country, activation of highly charged emotional memories is common.

As already mentioned, highly charged emotional memories do not always manifest in the form of visual images; they can also take the form of intrusive emotions and body sensations. In a very real way your body continues to operate on an entirely different set of assumptions than your ego. Van der Kolk again: "Although people with PTSD tend to deal with their environment through emotional constriction, their bodies continue to react to certain physical and emotional stimuli as if there were a continuing threat of annihilation; they suffer from hypervigilance, exaggerated startle response, and restlessness."[17] Hypervigilance is the result of our fight/flight/freeze response being on all of the time, despite the fact that we may not be aware that the switch has been flipped. I can still remember learning to listen intently to the footsteps above my room as a child, to discern whether they were friendly or dangerous, whether I could relax or should run. As a result, even today, certain footsteps will send electricity up my spine. The experience of hypervigilance requires a great deal of energy. Besides the constant visual/emotional/kinesthetic scanning of other people to determine their level of threat, our bodies continue to react to certain physical and emotional stimuli as if there were a continuing threat of annihilation.

Have you ever caught yourself jumping at even slight sounds and movements? That's a symptom of an exaggerated startle response. You can sometimes feel like a gun ready to go off at the slightest provocation. Van der Kolk writes "Perhaps the most distressing aspect of this hyperarousal is the generalization of threat. The world increasingly becomes an unsafe place: Innocuous sounds provoke an alerting startle response; trivial cues are perceived as indicators of danger."[18]

---

[15] *Ibid,* page 9

[16] *Ibid,* page 13

[17] *Ibid,* page 13

[18] *Ibid,* page 13

One of the unfortunate results of an exaggerated startle response is that our autonomic nervous system loses the capacity to accurately assess threat and serve as a guide for appropriate action. "The persistent, irrelevant firing of warning signals causes physical sensations to lose their functions as signals of emotional states," according to Van der Kolk, "and, as a consequence, they stop serving as guides for action."[19] When we're not able to trust our body-mind to guide our emotional reactions we can begin to feel deeply lost and frightened. We're truly "strangers in a strange land." The experience of overload can cause self-fragmentation that can be experienced as discontinuity in time and space.

(5) [T]hey suffer from generalized problems with attention, distractibility and stimulus discrimination…[20]

Problems with maintaining attention and staying focused are often some of the first indications of Compassion Fatigue. To be focused means to have clarity, to be present in the here and now, in your body experience, where reality actually occurs. Losing focus is often the first indicator that we aren't consciously tuned in to our body and reality. It often manifests as spacing out, obsessing, or dissociating. We find it difficult to sit quietly with ourselves and concentrate on any one task, thought, or feeling, or we might find ourselves constantly ruminating or stewing internally and having problems with short-term memory, concentration, and following through with tasks (such as completing chart work).

People with PTSD have difficulty in sorting out relevant from irrelevant stimuli; they have problems ignoring what is unimportant and selecting only what is most relevant. Easily over-stimulated, they compensate by shutting down.

— Bessel Van der Kolk, *Traumatic Stress,* page 14

In today's highly competitive work environment, care providers are being required to fulfill numerous roles and functions, to multi-task. The experience of multi-tasking can feel exactly like fighting multiple opponents simultaneously. Over a period of time the ability to distinguish the relevant from the irrelevant is compromised; everything becomes a crisis, resulting in system overload and eventual shut down. This loss of stimulus discrimination often results in a loss of flexibility, in being able to acquire new information and behaviors to respond spontaneously and creatively to new challenges. Van der Kolk, in *Traumatic Stress,* explains that "loss of flexibility may explain current findings of deficits in preservative learning and interference with acquisition of new information, as well as an inability to apply working memory to salient environmental stimuli."[21]

The progressive loss of emotional and even physical flexibility over time is the result of cumulative trauma that can take root in your body as an ongoing freeze response. Because of the under-activation of the neo-cortex and the over-activation of the sympathetic nervous system, along with the amygdala, new information is not learned and applied to current challenges. Traumatic stress really can make us stupid!

A participant at a recent seminar described her distraction like this: "I know I'm beginning to get Compassion Fatigue when I just can't concentrate. No matter how hard I try I can't get my mind to focus where and when I want it to. It's as though my brain has a mind of its own. I find myself daydreaming just minutes after I scold myself for daydreaming. Trying to concentrate is a joke! And forget memory!"

Another participant told me "The way I recognize distraction is when I can't focus anymore on my **patient**. It's as though there is so much noise going on in my own head I can't hear what my patient is saying. Sometimes it can get so bad that I have to stop the session and collect myself."

And one nurse manager explained "Sometimes I just want to spit! I get so frustrated with people, staff, and patients that I'm afraid I'll say or do something I'll regret later. At the end of the day I feel like I've been in a fight with 10 people at once. I feel exhausted but can't sleep, I'm physically sore in my shoulders, neck, and back and my mind keeps replaying certain scenes over and over. All I want to do is escape."

---

[19] *Ibid,* page 13

[20] *Ibid,* page 9

[21] *Ibid,* page 14

(6) *[T]hey have alterations in their psychological defense mechanisms and in personal identity. This changes what new information is selected as relevant…*[22]

When our core or nuclear self begins to break down we can experience severe anxiety or panic; it's the terror of fragmentation and annihilation. "Trauma," Van der Kolk explains, "is usually accompanied by intense feelings of humiliation; to feel threatened, helpless, and out of control is a vital attack on the capacity to be able to count on oneself. Shame is the emotion related to having let oneself down."[23] Shame entails the red-faced exposing of not just what we do, but who we are. In this capacity, there's no escape from shame. It doesn't matter what you do to feel better about yourself because your sense of guilt and badness has infiltrated its way to your core sense of self. It's with you wherever you go, whatever you do. Your usual defense mechanisms are inadequate to keep out this kind of threat.

To cope with the painful intrusions of shame we employ a "primitive" defense mechanism called projection, considered primitive because it's associated with earlier levels of development, with the infant or young child throwing up or throwing out "bad food" or those emotional experiences that are experienced as "contaminated" with self-badness. Projective identification is a term for disowning those parts of ourselves that we're ashamed of and identifying them in other persons, groups, or organizations. When we have a strong and sudden emotional reaction of fear, anger, or hatred to what we identify as a bad trait in others, this is an almost sure indication that we're reacting to a despised and disowned trait within ourselves. As the experience of ongoing shame threatens to crumble or shatter a weakening sense of self, we're incapable of taking responsibility or ownership of those parts of ourselves that we have judged from past experience to be intolerable. We simply can't take in and "metabolize" self-damning experiences. Instead, we must push them out onto other people, groups, or organizations.

The very act of projecting parts of ourselves onto others is one of splitting. Splitting is sometimes regarded as the hallmark defense mechanism of borderline personality disorders, although I believe

---

[22] *Ibid,* page 9

[23] *Ibid,* page 15

People with PTSD…

have problems ignoring

what is unimportant and

selecting only what is

most relevant.

— Bessel Van der Kolk,
Traumatic Stress, page 14

this is unfair and inaccurate. Everybody employs splitting to some degree. It's the matter of degree and perspective that's important. We can usually see splitting at work in organizations where there's an "in-group" and an "out-group," where there's more awareness of and emphasis on division and differences between others rather than similarities and common ground. Splitting is also at the root of most prejudices and is almost always involved in acts of violence toward others.

Reverting to earlier or primitive defense mechanisms will eventually create alterations in a person's personality structure. The more of your self feels intolerable to you the more you must split off and project it away. This is of course an illusory experience, as we can never really get rid of a part of ourselves. The result of this continued splitting and projecting is a continuing weakening in the core sense of self.

Changes in Personal Identity

The hallmark of vicarious traumatization is disrupted frame of reference. One's identity, world view, and spirituality together constitute frame of reference. As a result of doing trauma work, therapists are likely to experience disruptions in their sense of identity (sense of oneself as man/woman, as helper, as mother/father or one's customary feeling states), world view (moral principles, ideas about causality, life philosophy), and meaning and hope (sense of connection with something beyond oneself, awareness of all aspects of life, and sense of the non-material).

— B. Hudnall Stamm, *Secondary Traumatic Stress,* page 54

Over a period of time, untreated secondary traumatization will eventually create compensating structures in the personality as an adaptive function for the growing deterioration of one's sense of self. Essentially, the more we experience an erosion in our "sense of being an independent center of initiative and perception, integrated with our most central ambitions and ideals and with our experience that our body and mind form a unit in space and a continuum in time," the more distorted our self-perception will become. Progressive self-misperception will eventually lead to disruptions in our sense of identity, worldview, and spirituality.

Sense of Identity

For many care providers, our sense of personal identity is often intertwined with our identity as a helper. While this has some distinct advantages, including being able to empathize with our patients, it can lead to self-devaluation and eventually threaten our sense of self when we do not receive the kind of personal recognition or satisfaction we believe we deserve. As our sense of professional worthiness erodes under the continual demands and pressures of the job, our personal sense of "enoughness" is also threatened. The less worthy you feel, the less "good enough" you experience yourself to be. As your sense of enoughness erodes, the very foundation of your sense of identity is shaken; rather than your job being something you do, it becomes who you are. This shift from doing your job to being your job creates a condition in which you must meet your personal needs through your interactions as a care provider. This shift is often silent and invisible. We may truly have no clue that our perception has shifted. From our perspective, it's everybody else that has changed. We feel victimized and create or fall into situations in which we continue to be so, or victimize others.

World View

As our sense of identity shifts, our perceptions of others and of ourselves shift. We may increasingly find ourselves feeling separate and isolated from the rest of the world and develop a sense that something may be deeply "wrong" or "bad" with us, a feeling that can manifest as a need-desire to feel special and better than others with accompanying expectations of entitlement. This split between feeling especially bad and especially entitled is the result of a weakening sense of self. The weaker or more fragile you experience your core self to be, the more special and entitled you must feel about yourself and the more expectations you have that others should perceive you in the same way. It's a matter of balance. The worse you feel about yourself, the more you must have others respond to you in the way you need and expect in order to maintain homeostasis. This strategy, however, is faulty as it relies on perceiving yourself in greater misalignment with others as well as greater incongruence within yourself. The greater the misalignment and incongruence, the more likely you'll respond inaccurately and inappropriately to life events resulting in greater separateness and isolation. Eventually this process will expand to include coworkers, patients, family, friends, and community.

Spirituality

Broadly speaking, I'd like to define spirituality as our personal sense of connection with a benevolent life force larger than ourselves. It's what gives us a sense of inner belonging and direction, and this is exactly what begins to break down under the ever-pressing force of self-splitting. In order to have a sense of connection and belonging, it's first necessary to perceive ourselves as the very small yet essential, temporary yet valuable, individual yet connected beings that we really are. It's a matter of your point of view. If you view yourself as special/separate from the planet Earth, with the world revolving around *you,* for *your* personal need-desires, you're automatically cut off from any sense of belonging and connectedness. Those traits require, as a prerequisite, a view of yourself more in alignment with how the planet might see you. Think about it: the earth is big and relatively permanent. In comparison, we're small, temporary, and individual, nothing more than a flicker among many billions of others, a mere flash in time. The time and energy we spend on maintaining our "individuality" could be better spent on developing a sense of community and connection.

Chapter Four:

Your Body's Mind

The body is the unconscious mind! Repressed trauma
caused by overwhelming emotion can be stored in a
body part, thereafter affecting our ability to feel that
part or even move it. The new work suggests there
are almost infinite pathways for the conscious mind to
access — and modify — the unconscious mind and
the body, and also provide an explanation for a
number of phenomena that the emotional theorists
have been considering.

— Candace Pert, *Molecules of Emotion*, page141

Introduction

Researchers have recently been asking the question of whether the body could actually be a part of the unconscious mind, and a source of repressed trauma, whether the body could actually store traumatic memories, experiences, and emotions, and wondering what other functions the body might have in terms of regulating or calming our emotional states. Does your body play a role in all of these activities? What about awareness and intelligence: does your body have its own kind of sensing and knowing? If so, is it possible to access or tune in to the conversations your body-mind is having? In *Molecules of Emotion,* Dr. Candace Pert, a former research scientist for the National Institute of Health and now a Research Professor in the Department of Physiology and Biophysics at Georgetown University Medical Center, writes that "Full consciousness must involve awareness of not just mental but emotional and even basic physical experiences as well. The more conscious we are, the more we can 'listen in' on the conversation going on at autonomic or subconscious levels of the body-mind, where basic functions such as breathing, digestion, immunity, pain control, and blood flow are carried out."[1] Dr. Pert's findings are recent, but they confirm what's been a centerpiece of Chinese medicine and martial arts for thousands of years. The western world is only now just beginning to wake up to ancient knowledge.

The importance of the mind-body connection in helping to explain physical and emotional illness, as well as optimal states of health and performance, is finally being taken seriously enough to attract the attention and the pocketbook of the federal government, along with some significant private foundations. A recent article, "The New Science of Mind & Body" in *Newsweek,* September 27, 2004, illustrates this growing trend. According to *Newsweek,* the federal government is now engaged in a five-year-old Integrated Neural Immune Program that will spend 16 million dollars on mind-body research this year. Private foundations expect to spend millions more.

The idea that the body may have a mind of its own also has its roots in psychoanalytic theory. Freud had explained that the body and mind worked in conjunction as part of his theory of drives. Clearly the idea has been around for a while, but it's just now gaining mass acceptance within the health care community. In providing seminars on Post Traumatic Stress Disorder and

Compassion Fatigue across the United States, I've had the opportunity to interact with thousands of healthcare professionals who are often on the front line working with trauma survivors and who themselves are survivors of physical, sexual, or emotional trauma. What I hear more and more often from these treatment professionals are testimonials of how incomplete talk therapy is by itself, and how critical it is to address the body as a primary source of information. One social worker who worked with traumatized firemen from Ground Zero after the September 11th attacks told me that "Very often these firemen who witnessed unspeakable horror could not find any words to describe their experience. Some of them had gaps in their memory, others experienced dissociation, feeling as though they were outside of their body, watching the whole event from a distance. Others began to develop somatic symptoms: aches, cramps in their stomach, hypertension, buxism, one even had a heart attack. It was like their body was speaking for them." For trauma therapists, trauma survivors, and survivor caregivers, the concept of a body-mind as the center of experience, memories, emotions, even intuition and information, opens new horizons for discovery, relief, and mastery.

Body Memory

The idea that the body can actually "remember" traumatic events the ego can't is the foundation of trauma therapy. This type of memory is called somatic memory. More and more we're finding out that the body and brain are connected through a system of neurochemical transmitters that snap information back and forth between these two parts of the self. We're starting to see that there's less and less of a distinction between the brain and the body. They both comprise the self.

---

[1] Candace Pert, *Molecules of Emotion,* page 286

The Sensory System

The sensory system may be responsible for the most basic type of memory, as all experiences begin with sensory input from both our internal and external environments. The exteroceptors are nerves that transmit and receive information to and from the external environment through the five senses. Interceptors are the nerves that transmit and receive information from inside the body. Both play a role in how traumatic memories are laid down. The interoceptive system is responsive to stimuli emanating from inside the body that can be broken down into the proprioception and the vestibular sense. Proprioception can again be divided into the kinesthetic sense and the internal sense.

The Vestibular Sense

The vestibular sense is essential to body memory because it underlies our most basic sense of self, our sense that, to paraphrase Kohut, our body and mind form a unit in space and a continuum in time. It's the physical/emotional/perceptual sense of balance that's experienced when mind and body are connected and coordinated. Vestibular dysfunction, recent research suggests, can be triggered by such seemingly slight stimuli as adopting a certain stance or breathing pattern that you took during the time of certain traumatic events. Doctors who studied the psycho-somatic effects of whiplash or car crashes on people have found that certain bracing head movement patterns can re-activate an old traumatic body memory that can actually affect the vestibualar sense enough to re-experience vertigo. In the case of Compassion Fatigue or secondary traumatic stress, continual, repeated re-activation of the body's freeze response — tightened neck and shoulders and restricted breath — can reactivate old traumatic stress reactions, which then re-activate the body's freeze response, thereby creating a vicious cycle.

The understanding of body memory is also concerned with the interoceptive system that responds to stimuli from inside your body, particularly the kinesthetic and internal senses. People who

Full consciousness must involve awareness of not just mental but emotional and even basic physical experiences as well.

— Candace Pert, *Molecules of Emotion*, page 286

experience Compassion Fatigue often have difficulty sensing and utilizing valuable information that's encoded in the body more as a sense-feeling than in thoughts or words.

The Kinesthetic Sense

The kinesthetic sense is the root to almost all athletic ability, including martial arts. It's the sense of where each of your body parts are and what they're doing, bearing responsibility for connection, coordination, and responsiveness in your physical movements. It's more than just athletic ability, having been identified as a type of body intelligence, and it's a trait that, research suggests, all people possess. In many ways it's actually "smart" to be connected to your body. Your body really is the first, most direct source of information from your immediate physical environment. "Sensing" the emotions of others, utilizing empathy, is actually a refinement and extension of your sensory system.

People with Compassion Fatigue and other forms of traumatic stress often feel that they're in pieces, fragmented and disjointed. They often have chronic tightness, soreness, stiffness, and inflexibility in the body. They can feel uneasy and uncomfortable in their bodies and uncoordinated in their movements. There's often the sense that the body is a collection of individual pieces that, for the most part, have a mind of their own. They lack self-cohesion and connection with their internal sense. However, through the practice of FlowMotion™ described in the later chapters, you can become progressively aware of, and connected with, each part of your body separately and as a fluid, cohesive whole. Developing conscious body awareness and a sense of mindful movement are actually ways to increase your body-kinesthetic IQ.

The Internal Sense

Your internal sense is your body's equivalent to your emotional sense of self, enabling the perceptual-emotional sense of coherence and continuity in time and space as a whole and connected self. A stable, coherent internal sense is often something we take for granted, until we experience the disorganizing and fragmenting effects of traumatic stress. When you experience self-cohesion, there's an internal sense of safety, calm, connectedness, balance. When you experience chronic frozen-in-fear residual traumatic stress, there's an internal sense of fragmentation, of disintegration. The internal sense is also responsible for being able to identify and name emotions. It's the ability to listen inwardly, to sense and feel where and what in your body you're experiencing, and to translate the sensory experience into the cognitive recognition of that experience as an emotion.

Caregivers with Compassion Fatigue not only begin to lose access to, and connection with, their internal feeling states, they also experience misalignment in how they perceive themselves internally and how their actions and attitudes appear to others externally. Through repeated re-exposure to traumatic *Energy* in *MOTION*, caregivers can begin to lose their internal sense of self, their sense of self-coherence, and their sense of self-continuity. Who they are becomes misaligned with what they're doing. One care provider put it like this: "I didn't even realize that I was burning out until a good and trusted friend sat me down one day and spelled it out. She said I had changed since taking a job at the nursing home. She said I had become hardened, withdrawn, and my humor had become dark and macabre. She said I was always putting down my co-workers and supervisors and was constantly talking about what happened to my patients. She told me she saw me burning out. Strange thing is, I never noticed it until she told me."

The Severed-Self

One of the most devastating residual effects of secondary traumatic stress is the progressive freezing of, and dissociation from, our physical bodies. Through continual re-exposure to trauma and secondary trauma, the body goes into a habitual freezing response, resulting in chronic dissociation. Chronic, habitual dissociation can result in being almost completely absent from the experience of being inside and connected with your immediate physical sensations, impressions, hunches, and intuitions. It also results in being a captive of the ego. The ego is *not* the same thing as the rational mind, although it likes to parade in that disguise. The ego (as I'm using it here) is the self-serving, self-centered, entitled portion of our conscious and unconscious mind that's (secretly) connected to our hidden, despised, and devalued self.

The ego is the first one to point the finger at someone else for the very same projected quality that it secretly and shamefully recognizes within its own split, unconscious nature. That quality is the dark double that the ego doesn't want to admit about itself, but which, in reality, follows it around like a shadow, and permeates the rest of the self with its own negative energy as it lurks around behind the scenes. I like to consider this part of the ego as the severed-self.

Development of the Severed-Self

The severed-self is a very appropriate description for that part of our body-mind that's hidden in shame and fear. The term represents a split in the self as well as a part of the self that resides in pain, hurt, and enfeeblement due to emotional and possibly physical injuries of the past. In the case of traumatic stress, the pain is often the result of insult and injury; not only is there the pain of physical, emotional, and spiritual injury, there's often the insulting sense that it was self-caused and deserved.

The severed-self is actually comprised of accumulated traumatic energy-information that gets recorded as "energy-residue" in the nervous system and the very cells of our tissues. When we take in emotions, we take in energy; the neural-hormones that rush from the brain course through every cell in our bodies and leave an imprint of the experience of that emotion on the cells. New cells grow, following in the footsteps made by the old cells, reinforcing receptivity to the same emotions that carved a path through the old cells. So if we take in enough traumatic stress, enough traumatic experiences, those experiences literally become biologically encoded in the cell tissue, resulting in the formation of "cellular memory" that's both physical and emotional.

Physical body memory is often held as a particular body position and is recorded as vestibular memory. With some survivors, just taking

a particular stance or body position in conjunction with muscle and breath constriction can precipitate an eruption of traumatic stress. Traumatic memories can also be recorded as a type of informational energy exchange between body and mind. In *Molecules of Emotion,* Dr. Pert notes that "The emotions are the informational content that is exchanged via the psychosomatic network with the many systems, organs and cells participating in the process. Like information then, the emotions travel between the two realms of mind and body, as the peptides and their receptors in the physical realm, and as the feelings we experience and call emotions in the nonmaterial realm."[2]

In the severed-self this emotional-informational energy can be emblazoned upon the nervous system as the result of a traumatic experience and accumulate over time as less traumatic, and often ignored, continually repeated physical/emotional shocks. The body experiences a freeze response and the mind dissociates. Freezing isn't the only response to traumatic stress, either. The manifestation of simultaneous body and mind responses to traumatic stress, and the reminders of traumatic stress, have a range of expressions, from classic full physical paralysis and out-of-body dissociation, to less dramatic, and less noticeable, "body shocks" and obsessive internal pre-occupation, fantasy, or day-dreaming. Traumatic stress can accumulate as body memory as the result of continual, repeated body shocks that can adversely affect the kinesthetic and internal sense.

Caregivers who have already incorporated early traumatic stress into body memory are more vulnerable to experiencing disruption in their kinesthetic and internal sense as the result of continual, repeated body shocks they experience in their role as care providers, particularly if they're working with trauma survivors who are (re-)experiencing traumatic stress similar to theirs. The repeated and continual release of adrenaline to even minor, often unconscious, reminders of trauma can manifest as a type of feedback loop.

Care providers who have experienced traumatic stress in their own histories, particularly if the "frozen residue" of that traumatic stress has not been consciously re-integrated into the fabric of the self, are more vulnerable to continual re-freezing and dissociation. Recent research into Post Traumatic Stress Disorder has shown that the self

---

[2] Candace Pert, *Molecules of Emotion,* page 261

can't make the distinction between virtual and actual trauma. When the body and mind work in conjunction to combat a threat, neither the body nor mind stops to determine the immediacy of the threat. Memory, as well as clues taken from the external environment, prepare the body and the brain with rushes of hormones, triggering a reaction in the amygdala that perpetuates the reaction. This part of the brain, at this time, only understands the underlying message, "threat," and works to pump more hormones back into the body, regardless of whether the threat is real or imaginary. The body becomes aroused by fear and sends signals back to the amygdala, and we have a classic short circuit working that eventually congeals into a freeze-response.

This continual, repeated freezing-dissociation response takes its toll upon the awareness and responsiveness of the kinesthetic and internal sense, the body, and the intrapersonal intelligence. The body becomes increasingly rigid and inflexible, unable to feel whole, coherent, and integrated. Body parts can feel isolated, uncoordinated, even detached from the whole. Increasingly there's a sense of internal dis-ease, fragmentation, and disconnection. The sensation of intuition or "gut feeling" is drowned out by the repetitive undischarged freeze response, or body-shocks. The repeated body-shocks accumulate in the body and can activate emotional kindling, severely restricting the kinesthetic and internal senses. Simultaneously, the mind goes into a state of dissociation often resulting in derealization, a state that, when held over long periods of time, often manifests as a kind of unreality and "mental fog." The research into PTSD has shown that sufferers tend to lose their sense of selves, often feeling as though the life they live isn't recognizable, is somehow some kind of alien experience rather than a fully integrated life.

Dissociation affects how you perceive the world, sometimes even long after the traumatic event itself. Trauma can stick around in the body for years, resurfacing from time to time as a kind of somatic flashback of depersonalization, or even laying dormant within the body to be triggered for a first time long down the road, resulting in abnormal behaviors or other mental symptoms that can't be easily explained away by normal everyday stressors. Depersonalization, dissociation, and PTSD seem more and more as if they go hand in hand. Dissociation can also manifest as the inability to "metabolize" external experiences into internal structure because the emotion or *Energy in MOTION* of traumatic stress is "dis-integrating" rather than connecting. Integration requires the free exchange and circulation of energy and informa-

tion. Dissociation is the result of freezing, constricting, and isolating energy-information to a split-off, restricted fragment of the whole body-mind.

With greater fragmentation, experiences and even perception become increasingly isolated and disconnected. Peter Levine proposed one model that finds that during some point in the traumatic event, elements of the experience itself become disconnected. This SIBAM model of dissociation proposes that the Sensation, Image, Behavior, Affect, and Meaning of certain traumatic experiences can become fragmented, disconnected, and disintegrated from the normally whole mind-body perception. The result can be a chronic misinterpretation of events that leads to increased self-fragmentation and sensitivity to ordinary life stresses that then become misinterpreted and recorded in body memory as trauma.

At a recent Compassion Fatigue workshop a hospice case manager reported "Sometimes I can feel so fragmented on the inside, that everything I experience on the outside is also in pieces. It's like trying to view your life in the reflection of a mirror that's been broken into bits; everything you see is also in pieces." Trauma can literally break your world, inside and out, turning both internal reality and external reality into distorted, cracked, shattered experiences.

Your Core Center

The concept of a "core center," as used here, draws from the traditional Eastern perspective utilized in martial arts. From this standpoint, the martial arts standpoint, the core center is a well-known, accepted, and demonstrable concept of dynamic equilibrium that develops as a student finds his or her center, also known as the Tan-tien. In *Movements of Magic*, Bob Klein offers a good working definition of this concept. "Every level of being — molecular, cellular and organic — is coordinated by the Tan-tien," he writes. "The Tan-tien is the center of harmony among all your individual parts. By sinking your attention into this level, you are placing the body's fulcrum at the center of harmony and thus empowering it."[3]

---

[3] Bob Klein, *Movements of Magic,* page 28

The core center is a place within your body-mind that you experience right in the center of your being and that contains your innermost core sense of self. Physically it's felt to be about three to four inches below your naval in the center of your body. If you close you eyes and sense your most central, inside your body experience of awareness, balance, focus, and equilibrium you should be getting close to your core. You may even sense a feeling of recognition, like you just came home.

The core center is that place you sometimes feel deep in your "guts" that gives you invaluable, intuitive advice. It is the place you attune your attention to when you're listening to your "gut feelings" to get a sense of the emotions that you or others currently experience. When nourished, the core center flourishes. In martial arts, the core center is essential for all movement, as every breath and motion initiated, as well as all power and connection, begin from there. Even a sense of connection with your sparring partner that directs your movement emanates from your core.

Many care providers with Compassion Fatigue have a sense of weakness or fragility within their core sense of self, and because this is an area of the severed-self that can retain traumatic memories, many caregivers avoid placing their attention or feeling there. But the core center thrives on attention energy. When it's starved or cut off from this life-giving energy, it can dwindle, diminish, and atrophy.

The core center is the body-mind equivalent to the sense of self. The more you experience the conscious awareness in your core center, the more grounded, stable, coherent, and connected you experience your "self" to be. Eckhart Tolle writes in *Practicing the Power of Now* that "In this state of inner connectedness, you are much more alert, more awake than in the mind identified state. You are fully present. [Attention to the core] also raises the vibrational frequency of the energy field that gives life to the physical body."[4] Your core also has a connection with your body-kinesthetic and intrapersonal intelligence. The more aware and centered you are there, the more connected you are with the subtle signals and energy/information that are continually available to your conscious awareness.

The most telling sign that we're not paying much attention to the core center is the way in which we breathe. Martial artists understand fully that breath truly is the key to physical, emotional, and even mental power. In Gung-fu and Qigong breath is central to every movement, internal and external. Breath initiates, connects, directs, and controls every motion a martial artist makes. Most people who attend my Compassion Fatigue workshops intellectually recognize the importance of breath but very often fail to incorporate that recognition into their everyday practice of breathing. Most will admit that, at best, they breathe short, shallow breaths from the upper portion of their lungs while chronically squeezing, even freezing, the muscles of their diaphragm. One care provider wrote in after a recent workshop telling me "I realized after your talk why I have had tight stomach muscles all these years despite a lack of exercise. This has been from holding my breath/diaphragm for years! I was quite shocked when I realized this and now am finally breathing with my whole diaphragm/torso for perhaps the first time in decades! This has completely gotten rid of my TMJ as well as some stomach problems and general body tightness."

The Heart-Brain

The idea that the heart is intelligent is by no means a new idea. The ancient Greeks believed the heart was the true source of intelligence. Proverbs 23:7 declares "For as a man thinketh in his heart, so is he." The Chinese words for thinking, thought, intent, listening, virtue, and love all include the character for "heart." It's a symptom of intellectual arrogance to believe thought can be separated from emotion, feeling, and sensation. It's also a mistake in physiology. Recent research suggests that the nervous system has two different parts: the sympathetic branch, which works to make the heart go faster in response to certain emotional stimuli, and the parasympathetic branch, which makes the heart slow down when responding to other different stimuli. The anxious or agitated exhaustion so prevalent in people with Compassion Fatigue really is a state of being both "wired and tired." When the heart is engaged in a sympathetic response to a client expressing emotional pain, the sympathetic (aptly named) nervous system responds to the signals transmitted by the heart by producing adrenaline in preparation for fight/flight/freeze (the gas). The parasympathetic branch produces acetycholine that promotes states of relaxation (the brake).

---

[4] Eckhart Tolle, *Practicing the Power of Now,* page 20

Normally there's a balance between the sympathetic and parasympathetic branches of the nervous system, each of them working in harmony with the other toward the optimal state of "psychophysiological coherence." In *The Science of the Heart*, a book produced by the HeartMath Research Center, psychophysiological coherence is defined as:

"A state associated with:

- Sustained positive emotion

- High degree of mental and emotional stability

- Constructive integration of the cognitive and emotional systems

- Increased synchronization and harmony between the cognitive, emotional and physiological systems."[5]

As defined in this text, psychophysiological coherence definitely has the appearance of an optimal state, one that corresponds to the idea of flow.

It's my experience that practicing the physical movements of FlowMotion™ can immediately and significantly increase psychophysiological coherence. You can actually measure this state by measuring heart rate variability (HRV). Recent research suggests that a situation of equilibrium maintained by the two branches of the nervous system, the two parts that work to influence the heart, is the optimal mind-body state. When we're lost in flow, we become fully balanced.

When we're in the throes of Compassion Fatigue, and our sympathetic nervous system is pumping out adrenaline in response to the signals from our heart-brain, the HRV shows a pattern of chaos rather than coherence. When we're able to introduce a psychophysiological state of flow, the HRV shows a pattern of coherence. HeartMath at www.heartmath.org has been on the leading edge of some of the research being conducted that associates coherent HRV to optimal states of mental and emotional well-being. They have introduced a training program of interactive software they call the "Freeze Framer" that allows users to instantly observe their level of HRV coherence or "entrainment" as measured on a finger sensor that feeds this data directly to a computer program that displays the results instantly on your screen.

There are three levels of entrainment on the Freeze Framer program: low, medium, and high. High levels of entrainment are most associated with high levels of psychophysiological coherence: *sustained positive emotion, high degree of mental and emotional stability, constructive integration of the cognitive and emotional systems, and increased synchronization and harmony between the cognitive, emotional and physiological system.*

While HeartMath and others have studied the effect of psychophysiological coherence by focusing on your heart and inducing positive emotional states such as appreciation, I have not yet seen a study that measures coherence utilizing the mindful movement and conscious breathing techniques of FlowMotion™, so I conducted my own.

Utilizing the technology supplied by HeartMath, I compared my "normal" level of entrainment with my level of entrainment after 40 minutes of meditation and after five minutes of FlowMotion™ for 10 days. My "normal" or baseline entrainment was fairly consistent for the 10 days, showing a split in my level of entrainment. Out of a total possible 100 percent score for all three levels of entrainment, low, medium, and high, my baseline was between 60 to 80 percent low, 20 to 30 percent medium, and 0 to 10 percent high.

After 40 minutes of meditation my entrainment levels would shift to 30 to 50 percent low, 30 to 50 percent medium, and 10 to 30 percent high for the 10 days, indicating a slight improvement over time. After five minutes of FlowMotion™ my entrainment levels shot immediately to 15 percent medium and 85 percent high in the very first trial. For the next nine trials, the entrainment levels were pinned between 95 to 100 in the high range, and 0 to 5 in the medium range.

The practice of FlowMotion™ is the most direct method for achieving high levels of entrainment and coherence that I know of. By attuning your heart to the natural, gentle rhythms of your body-mind in flowing physical, mindful movement and conscious breathing, you will transform the frozen energy of Compassion Fatigue into the fluid energy of flow.

---

[5] HeartMath Research Center, *The Science of the Heart*, page 17

Chapter Five:

Your Most Precious Natural Resource

This power, developed through rooting, is intimately tied to breath. Throughout spiritual literature the world over, breath is highly regarded as a key to personal development and internal power.

— Bob Klein, *Movements of Magic*, page 9

Introduction: From Freezing to Flowing

Energy may very well be your most valuable natural resource, more valuable than even time. Taking personal responsibility for the quantity and quality of our personal *Energy in MOTION* is not always an easy thing to do. As already discussed, we often unconsciously employ dissociation, projection, and splitting as a result of trying to disown the severed-self. The more you try to get rid of a part of yourself, the more you unconsciously empower that part to operate independently of your central awareness, and the more your body feels like it has a mind of its own. It's this state of incoherence in which head, heart, and gut are out of alignment.

The first step to transforming frozen energy into flowing energy is to have an honest look at where our energy leaks and energy blocks are. This can be tough to do because we get so accustomed to blaming external events or people for the quality and quantity of our personal energy that we become emotionally convinced that we truly are the victims of circumstance. Reclaiming our personal energy really is reclaiming disowned and devalued parts of our own self.

The central method for reclaiming your energy is to become aware of your breathing. Breath really is energy. It may be just as simple as that. When you really begin to focus your attention inside your body for longer and longer periods of time, you will begin to become aware of just how often and in which circumstances you tense the muscles of your neck and shoulders and hold your breath. As you begin to notice this you can systematically train your body to relax and breathe.

As you begin to breathe consciously you'll notice how different you feel, physically, emotionally, mentally, and even spiritually. Physically, your energy will begin to transform from the nervous, jittery, adrenaline rush associated with tense, shallow breathing to a more relaxed, even, and flowing energy associated with long, slow, deep breathing. Emotionally, you'll begin to feel more balanced, centered, and connected to your core center. Mentally you'll begin to experience greater clarity, and spiritually you may begin to sense more connection with others and with a force larger than yourself.

Energy Leaks

Energy leaks occur when your attention and intention are out of alignment with what's occurring in your here and now, in-your-body reality. When unresolved traumas of the past are triggered by perceived danger in the present, fear and uncertainty are projected into the future. Your presence, which is the result of being present in your body, is splintered, weakened, and fragmented. The greater the fragmentation, the more energy leakage you have.

Energy leaks are often very subtle and usually occur when you're not fully conscious or feeling centered and connected inside your body, when you're unconsciously stewing, or obsessing about something that has either already happened or not yet happened. The more intense and emotionally charged the stewing, the more your body produces powerful hormonal stimulants in response to the mental images you're watching, and the more likely a mind/body short circuit will occur. Your body is all dressed up for fight or flight and has nowhere to go.

You can consciously experience this condition physically. Hold both hands out in front of you and press your right palm flat against your left as if you were going to pray. Make sure your elbows are sticking out, so that your forearms form a straight line. Begin to press your right palm against your left as hard as you possibly can. What's your natural response? For most of us it's automatic to counteract the force of our right palm by pressing back with the left. Continue to increase the pressure, right pushing on left and left pushing back on right. Now what begins to happen? Can you feel the tension move from your hands into your arms, shoulders, and chest? How about into your neck and jaw? Continue to apply pressure and begin to imagine that one hand must win against the other. Both hands believe that they alone, in their own isolated reality, are completely and absolutely right. Each hand must win: it's life and death! Where's the tension now? Can you feel the restriction of your breath?

Now let off the pressure and take a deep breath. Feel a little tired? In a state of stress, your intention and attention work like your left and right hands just did. You may want to focus on one thing, but external pressures force your focus onto something else. These two aspects of your personality go into conflict and contradiction, draining the body of its resources.

Holding It All In

In addition to energy leaks, we also have energy blocks. Energy blocks are a result of a third type of unconscious response to the experience of chronic danger, the freeze response. When some of us are confronted with repetitive primary and secondary traumatic stress, especially when we're powerless to exert a direct effect upon the source of that stress, rather than fight or flee, we're more likely to shut down and freeze.

Energy blocks are often experienced as "dead zones" in the body where, at first glance, there appears to be a numbing lack of energy and awareness. On closer examination these dead zones are more like "emotional black holes," because the emotion is buried deep in the tissue as body memory. This buried emotion is often traumatic, comprised of partial, fragmented and whole images, body sensations, and sound bites that appear frozen in time.

Energy blocks can result from many kinds of traumatic experiences including childhood physical, sexual, and emotional abuse and neglect, war and terrorism, or sudden emotional, financial, or physical losses. They can also result from the accumulation of unresolved and un-discharged stress that gets stored away. These blocks can be very deceptive and difficult to identify. They can lie dormant for years, silently siphoning off your physical, emotional and mental energy, until they're suddenly and intrusively activated by a current event that, on the surface, appears to have no relationship to the emotional distress you experience. You can suddenly become overwhelmed with primitive, raw emotions, sensations, and memory fragments that feel like they've been stuck in time. Even though they're past events, they seem to happen in the present.

Afraid to Breathe

One of the consequences of holding on to energy blocks is a holding of the breath. Those of us who have experienced trauma and traumatic stress in our lives know the best way not to feel is not to breathe. We're literally afraid to breathe.

Frozen breathing is like trying to breathe with a heavy weight on your chest. Without even recognizing it we take in very short, shallow, restricted breaths that aren't allowed to sink into the stomach or to circulate upward and touch the heart. Breathing equals feeling. When we breathe in and out with frozen breaths, we aren't able to absorb and circulate the oxygen throughout the body that's necessary to fully stimulate the muscles, nerves, and tissues. These parts are literally starved for oxygen and attention.

A restriction of oxygen is complementary to a restriction of awareness. Energy-oriented trauma therapists have known for some time that attention, the focus of our awareness, follows the energy of our breath. Where breath energy is restricted or blocked, so is awareness. Breath of Relief and the exercises in this book bring oxygen, energy, and awareness into your body by combining conscious breathing and mindful movement to discharge the frozen energy of traumatic stress and recharge your body with living, flowing breath energy.

Breath is Energy

Breath really is energy. Both the oxygen that's contained in breath, as well as the act of breathing itself, are primary sources of the body's energy. The rate and flow of the breath along with its depth, intensity, and rhythm, have a direct and immediate effect upon the type and amount of energy we feel.

Take a minute and breathe in a long, slow, deep breath from your diaphragm. Count to six on the in-breath, allow it to make a fluid transition to out-breath, and then gently push your breath all the way out from your diaphragm to a count of eight. Do this a couple of times. What did you experience?

Now try taking just a couple short, rapid, powerful breaths in through your nose, followed by an exhalation of oxygen from your mouth. Time the incoming breath to just two seconds. Consciously open your lower lung by pushing your abdomen in with your diaphragm as you inhale. Exhale forcefully up through your throat and out of your mouth as though you were to say "ah" without using your voice. Try just a couple of breaths and stop if you feel dizzy.

Can you feel a difference in the amount, type and intensity of energy you get from these different kinds of breathing?

Now take another minute just paying attention to your breath as you breathe naturally. Allow your breath to breathe itself. Relinquish the idea that you have to be in control of each breath. Give in to the sensation of allowing your breath to find its way into your lungs as you open your diaphragm to create a vacuum that naturally draws oxygen in. Allow your abdomen to extend without effort as your diaphragm expands.

Follow your breath with your attention as it flows into your lungs. Notice how tense or relaxed your abdomen muscles are as you breathe in. How far down in your diaphragm does your breath go? How tense are your chest and lungs as you fill them with oxygen? Notice the moment of transition between the end of an in-breath and the beginning of an out-breath. For just a brief moment the breath is effortless, weightless, and suspended in time. Allow your attention to hover in this zone during the transition. Can you feel the exquisite fullness of that moment?

Allow your breath to release itself, gently and fluidly, as you begin to exhale. Rather than pushing the breath out, imagine that the atmosphere outside of you is drawing the breath from your lungs. See if you can visualize yourself being breathed by the atmosphere outside of you. Surrender for just a moment your idea of individual will to the experience of being connected directly to your external environment by your breath.

The way you breathe directly and immediately impacts both the quality and quantity of your physical, emotional, mental, and spiritual energy. Breath is energy. It's by far our most precious natural resource and yet, for the most part, we tend to restrict, hold, or ignore it.

Physical Energy

Breath is the carrier of energy that's generated at the center of the body known as the "Tan Tien," or "core." When you learn to draw breath from and breathe into your core, you can breathe power and grace into your physical movements. The more time you spend breathing into the core, the stronger it becomes. Breath not only animates and energizes your physical movements, it also connects them. These fully connected physical movements appear effortless and fluid.

The idea that breath and physical energy are closely interwoven is known by every martial artist who has seriously studied the power of Qi (Chi), or Ki. Virtually every school of martial art has some kind of practice to harness and focus physical energy and power through specific breathing exercises, from the explosive "Ki-Yah!" of the Karate fighter to the more subtle and silent nourishing and circulating breath of Qi Gong practitioners. The advanced practice of most martial arts actually centers upon combining breath, energy, and motion into a seamless and fluid dance that carries the martial artist into different levels of awareness.

The way in which you breathe mirrors the quality of your physical energy. When you're tense, tight, and frozen in your physical energy, your breath will also be shallow, frozen, and restricted. When you feel drained and exhausted, your breath will be weak and without vigor. Experiment for yourself. Try moving in harmony with your breath by simply pulling your hand up from your lap with your in-breath and putting it back down with your out-breath. As you gently and deeply breathe in from your diaphragm, smoothly and fluidly raise your hand as if it were weightless and in total harmony with the rhythm of your in-breath. As your hand and breath simultaneously reach the apex of inhalation, allow a smooth and seamless transition from up to down, in to out, as your hand and breath finish the cycle and return to their original starting points.

Try another energy exercise. Draw in just half a breath as you simultaneously tighten every muscle in your arm and hand. At the same time, slowly, and with a sense of great effort, pull your frozen arm and hand up as you breathe in. As your hand stiffly reaches the apex of the motion immediately reverse direction, maintaining as much tension as possible in your hand and arm, and breathe out a short explosive breath.

Can you feel the difference in the quality and quantity of your physical energy? One of the fastest, most direct routes to controlling your energy is to control how you breathe. The more conscious you are of your breathing when you get stressed and tired, the more immediately you'll be able change your energy level by breathing consciously.

Emotional Energy

The way in which you breathe also immediately impacts your emotions. Anybody who has had a panic attack can tell you that anxiety and hyperventilation are two sides of the same process. Panic attacks are often precipitated by rapid, tense, shallow breathing and can immediately be soothed by taking longer, slower, deeper breaths. Emotions are *Energy* in *MOTION*. They're directly impacted by the quality of your breath, just as your breathing can be influenced by the quality of your emotions. It's a two-way street. Different emotions are associated with different rates, intensities, and rhythms of breathing.

Allow yourself to feel a pleasant, easy, relaxing emotion like serenity or peacefulness. Remember the last time you felt serene and at peace. Where were you? What was happening that caused you to feel that way? Visualize that situation and bring it closer to your experience. Notice your breathing. What's the rate of your breath? How deep, smooth, and connected is it? Can you allow your breath to mirror more closely your experience of serenity? Can you feel the convergence of breath and emotion?

Now allow yourself to experience the emotions associated with stress. Bring to mind the latest stressful (not traumatic) experience you've had and replay it as though it were happening again. What happened to get you so stressed out? As you replay the most stressful part of the experience, notice what happens to your breathing. Do you notice shallow, jerky in-breaths? Can you feel yourself

When you learn to draw breath from and breathe into your core, you can breathe power and grace into your physical movements.

unconsciously hold your breath in anticipation? Notice how your out-breath is released suddenly in uneven spurts.

Breath is almost continuously reflective of the emotions that we feel. If you were able to consciously observe your breath moment to moment for an extended period of time, you would notice how fluidly breath and emotion mirror each other.

Conscious breathing can influence your emotional state. In *Molecules of Emotion* Dr. Candace Pert writes that "Conscious breathing, the technique employed by both the yogi and the woman in labor, is extremely powerful. There is a wealth of data showing that changes in the rate and depth of breathing produce changes in the quantity and kind of peptides that are released from the brain stem."[1] Conscious breathing is more than just being conscious of your breath. It involves breathing with intent. Consciously breathing at a certain rate and intensity, especially when combined with visualization, can evoke a specific emotional response.

Give this exercise a try. Just begin to notice the breath that is still in your lungs even after exhaling. For most of us, our abdomens have become frozen and rigid from the accumulation of stress that we chronically hold in. Breath gets stuck at the bottom of the lungs. Notice how the oxygen doesn't really flush out at the end of the breath so that as you breathe in you're taking in less fresh oxygen.

Consciously exhale all of the air from your lungs by slowly and gently squeezing your diaphragm inward as you discharge the remainder of your breath. As your lungs become emptier and emptier imagine that you're discharging all of the accumulated frozen energy that has been trapped as stale oxygen and chronic stress. Imagine all of this energy being exhaled with your breath.

Imagine that the breath you take in is a stream of energy that you breathe into that area in your chest you feel as your emotional heart. Direct your attention to that spot as you take in a long, slow, tranquil breath from deep within your abdomen. As you breathe in follow your breath with your attention, starting from deep within your core. As your lungs open, imaginatively enter into the breath itself as it travels from your core through the center of your body-mind toward your heart.

Allow your attention to surround the place in your chest you experience as your emotional heart region. Sometimes people experience emotions right in the middle of the chest that are certainly heart-felt although not directly in the position of the physical heart. As your in-breath reaches its apex, imaginatively sense the energy of your breath surrounding, penetrating, and circulating through your emotional heart with its energy and intelligence. Consciously breathe energy in, through, and around your emotional heart. Experience the emotion that is generated by conscious breathing as you slowly and gently exhale.

One of the most pleasant and productive ways that you can invest two of your most precious natural resources, your time and energy, is to begin to pay conscious attention to your breathing when you experience positive emotions such as love, forgiveness, serenity, and appreciation.

Far too often we tend not to fully absorb and internalize many of our day-to-day energizing experiences because we're chronically mentally distracted, possessed by anxiety, fragmented by anger and rage, or escaping in fantasy. When uplifting and energizing events do happen we are often out of tune with feeling positive emotions and those that we do let in are not fully absorbed, celebrated, metabolized, and integrated into the heart of the Natural Self.

The next time you notice that you're in a positive mood, do yourself a giant favor and take just a few minutes to allow your attention to sink inside your body and center on your breathing. You don't really need to stop what you're doing, just bring some of your attention into the center of your body and let it rest there. There's no need to do anything different, just be there, aware.

Allow your awareness to focus on your breathing. Don't change how you breathe, just let your awareness rest there. With your in-breath imagine that you're breathing in, circulating, internalizing, and metabolizing the positive emotion that you currently feel. Visualize your positive emotion as pure energy that feeds and illuminates every cell in your body. As you exhale, visualize that you are connected and nourishing all living things outside your body with your positive *Energy in MOTION*.

---

[1] Candace Pert, *Molecules of Emotion,* page 186

Mental Energy

How do you define and describe mental energy? Is it just the energy required to process information in the brain? How much energy does that take? If oxygen is required to produce energy how much oxygen does the brain use? Even though the brain accounts for just 2 percent of the body's weight, it utilizes almost 25 percent of the body's oxygen. It's quite understandable how a steady, even, deep flow of oxygen to the brain is beneficial to clear thinking.

Try it out for yourself as you read. The next time you feel mentally fatigued, stop and put the book down. Sit quietly in a chair with a straight back and lay your hands in your lap. Allow your eyes to remain open and soften their gaze so that they take in images more as patterns and shapes of light and color than individual things.

Allow your abdomen to relax and let your breath discharge fully. Mentally follow your breath as it's discharged into the atmosphere around you. Can you visualize the heavy, cloudy feeling of fatigue being released from your brain as you exhale? Can you feel the muscles of your eyes and forehead relax as well?

Continue to breathe consciously. Just at the point where your out-breath changes to in-breath, notice the feeling of becoming emptier and emptier. Allow the spacious feeling of emptiness to enter imaginatively into your brain, clearing space for new refreshing and re-vitalizing energy.

Breathe in to a count of six and imagine that the energy of your breath is being directly absorbed into your mind. As the volume of your breath energy increases with inhalation, visualize it circulating and clearing away all of your mental fog. Imagine all of that fog dissipating, and slowly and smoothly discharge your breath to a count of eight.

Continue to breathe smoothly and fully in this way for at least three breaths. With each breath allow your mind to become clearer and more focused. After the third breath refocus your attention on reading the book.

How do you feel now after consciously breathing energy directly into your mind? Can you feel a sense of energy generated by having fully absorbed the oxygen of your breath and visualized the circulating, nourishing, revitalizing energy? Visualization is a well-known technique among coaches and sports psychologists to enhance performance and recovery and is well documented by Dr. Candace Pert in *Molecules of Emotion*. "Through visualization…," she writes, "we can increase the blood flow into a body part and thereby increase the availability of oxygen and nutrients to carry away toxins and nourish the cells."[2]

In addition to providing more energy, conscious breathing, especially when combined with visualization, can enhance the focus of your energy. Establishing, enhancing, and maintaining a clear focus are essential skills for all martial artists, whether you practice a physical form of martial art or whether you're an "interpersonal martial artist," as many care providers are. The ability to establish, enhance, and maintain a clear focus of mental energy on what you're doing in the here and now, in your body reality, is essential.

Conscious breathing is a deceptively difficult process. The moment your attention becomes settled and centered it'll be instantly coaxed away by all kinds of internal and external distractions. In fact, it can be quite a humbling experience when you give this next exercise a try with as much self-awareness as you can.

Begin by sitting in a comfortable chair with your back straight, eyes open, and your hands in your lap. Allow your breathing to become relaxed and take long, deep, even breaths. Consciously breathe deep into your core as you open your diaphragm and allow breath energy to sink into your lower abdomen. When you exhale, allow your abdomen to push all of the oxygen out completely to become as empty as possible. Allow your breathing to get into an easy, steady, natural rhythm.

When your breath has become steady and regular, focus your attention on an object in front of you. It can be any object. Allow your attention to absorb the image of that object as fully and completely as you can for one minute. Imagine that you're actually breathing the image of that object into your mind.

After the minute is up, close your eyes and reproduce the image of the object as completely and exactly as possible on the screen of

---

[2] *Ibid,* page 146

your mind. Try to capture every detail (size, shape, color, texture) of the object that you can on your brain's internal screen. Keep your attention focused only on the image of that object. If other thoughts, images, emotions, or body sensations distract your focus or take your attention away, bring them back to the image as soon as you notice.

Continue to focus your attention for as long as you can as you try to reproduce the image as exactly as possible in your mind's eye. What do you experience? Can you feel the energy of your focus begin to fade, dissolve, or splinter? Do you observe a succession, even intrusion, of thoughts or images, possibly even memories, into your awareness?

Now expand your awareness to include any tension you may be experiencing in your face, eyes, or shoulders. Are you holding or restricting your breath as you concentrate? Do you experience tension anyplace else in your body? What's it like to shift your attention from internal to external? How do you feel emotionally?

The ability to establish, nurture, and maintain a consciously focused attention is invaluable when investing mental energy into any task. As the previous exercise may have shown, you're routinely assaulted by multiple distractions, both internal and external, that seem to conspire to keep you distracted, that fragment your energy, focus, and attention.

Focusing and maintaining mental energy and cognitive capacity are intimately connected with body movement and exercise. When conscious breathing is integrated with mindful movement a synergy of awareness, breath, energy and motion is cultivated. The result is spiritual energy.

Spiritual Energy

The concept of spiritual energy is very difficult to define and is made more difficult by so many already existing definitions. For some it may include a connection with God, for others it may be more of an earthy, natural energy, and yet others may experience spiritual energy as a connecting energy that binds all things together. I still prefer the use of Qi or Chi, as the Chinese word for "life energy." Chi is the moving, flowing energy that resides in and emanates from every living thing on earth. According to most eastern ways of thought, the whole world is brought together through this living energy.

To experience spiritual energy consciously, we must let go of the ego, which maintains our over-riding sense of self-importance and self-absorption. What keeps us most isolated and cut off from the energy that's abundant and available is our sense of separation from the earth. Keep in mind, though, that we're never fully separate from the earth: we were born from it and we'll all return to it in the end.

The part of yourself that's most in touch with the earth is your physical self, your body, your breath and motion.

As I look back on the seemingly endless days and nights of black depression I myself have suffered, I wonder now how I could not have felt the energy that's all around us, pouring out of the sun and up from the earth, oozing from plants and radiating from trees. The more we're able to tune our awareness and become receptive to the energy that's all around us, the lighter, springier, more fluid, and alive we feel.

Qi or spiritual energy is both the energy we feel running through us as well as the energy that's external to us. They're two parts of the same whole. It is only when you're able to "lose your mind and come to your senses" that you'll allow yourself to acknowledge that which you already sense in your body. It's not even so much that you have to immerse yourself in a new concept or philosophy to experience Qi. Just let go of ideas and concepts that tend to hem in your awareness rather than allow it to expand. Qi is already there. Just let yourself feel it. Start internally, through your own body at first, then later you will recognize it and be able to consciously join with it, even navigate it, externally in your interactions with your environment and others.

The natural result of feeling more energy, conscious, aware, living, and intelligent energy, is a greater feeling of connectedness. Actually, it's more like allowing what's already real and true the full acknowledgement of that truth and reality, to recognize that we really, truly are connected to each other and to the earth. As you align your personal perception with this reality, a very interesting thing begins to happen. You develop a more powerful source of motivation, perseverance, and direction that feeds your passion, commitment, integrity, and honesty.

Try the following brief breathing and visualization exercise to get a sense of your connection with the Earth and with a sense of belonging and identity larger than your personal, individual self. Sit comfortably in a chair with your back straight and your feet squarely on the floor. Rest your hands on your abdomen and allow yourself to focus on your breath. As you breathe slowly, deeply, and evenly from your diaphragm, allow your awareness to focus on and into every part of the breathing motion itself. Consciously extend your abdomen on the in-breath to take in more oxygen, slowly expanding your lungs, and then release the oxygen evenly as you exhale.

Continue to focus on each and every movement of your lungs as you breathe in and out. Begin to notice subtle micro-movements that connect the larger more obvious movements. Notice how you can influence those movements just by how you draw in or release your breath.

Utilize your creative imagination and visualize that you're becoming smaller, smaller, and smaller so that you're the size of an oxygen molecule. Can you visualize yourself the size of a molecule? That's probably not a bad comparison of our size and importance relative to the universe. What would your perspective be like if you were the size of a molecule?

As an oxygen molecule imagine that you're being drawn in with your breath. What do you see? What would it be like to be one of billions of molecules being drawn into this immense living, intelligent, powerful being? What would the journey be like to be drawn into the lungs and blood cells, transported through the heart, around the body, and finally back to the lungs and out with the exhalation of breath? Can you imagine it?

After you're exhaled what happens as you're released back into the atmosphere? What's your sense of connection with other oxygen molecules? What's your connection with the sunlight, the trees, the wind? Can you feel yourself rushing with trillions of other oxygen molecules into and through the atmosphere? What's your perspective now? What can you see now as a single molecule that you couldn't see before as a human being?

Imagine, sense, and visualize that you're now part of a jet stream high above the earth, flowing, streaming, connecting. Imagine that besides just your individual identity as a single oxygen molecule, you also share the identity and experience of every other oxygen molecule as well. You're both here and there, in one place and many simultaneously. What's your experience of connection now?

Allow yourself to completely return to your here and now reality by focusing on your breath, feeling the weight in your hands, your feet on the ground.

I believe spiritual energy really is the energy that connects and empowers all life. To experience spiritual energy you must be continually willing to let go of the need to be right, special, or better than others, self-important and self-absorbed. You must be continually willing to take yourself out of the center of the universe and begin to view life in a more objective way, to acknowledge that as an individual you're very small and insignificant in the larger scheme of things.

When you're humble enough to perceive your true size and importance in context of even just this planet, not to mention the universe, you can (re-)align your energy, attention, and intention with a more coherent, laser beam focus. The key is becoming more conscious and aware of your breath, which is your energy.

Energy really is your most valuable natural resource of physical, emotional, mental, and spiritual energy. Conscious breathing is the key to experiencing more energy. As I hope the exercises demonstrated, how you breathe is intimately connected with the amount and type of energy you experience moment to moment. When conscious breathing is combined with aware, present, mindful movement, the result is a release, circulation and transformation of frozen, stuck *Energy* in *MOTION* into living, flowing, nurturing energy.

Chapter Six:

Mindful Movement

It begins by connecting all parts of the body in a
coherent, unified flow of motion... Thus your body
and all its parts, the attention, momentum and breath
are all connected and flowing together as one unit.

— Bob Klein, *Movements of Magic*, pages 11-12

Introduction

In combination with conscious breathing, mindful movement collects, refines, amplifies, aligns, and focuses *Energy in MOTION*. Mindful movement is any kind of fully conscious motion that's done in harmony with your breathing and in alignment with the spontaneous expression and evolution of your Natural Self for the enjoyment and mastery of creative motion.

Mindful movement is natural movement, a physical flow that creatively expresses the essence of the Natural Self. The harder you try to do mindful movement, the more difficult it becomes. The more you surrender to the natural rhythm that's already playing within your body and mind, the more natural and spontaneous your motions become. Such motions are centered and connected, beginning in your core, flowing up through the center of your body, and bringing all of your parts together in motion and rhythm, while still remaining anchored to your core.

Each part of your body is separate, with its own individual awareness and intelligence, and simultaneously connected, immediately responsive to every other part of your body. No part of your body moves in complete isolation. Every movement influences and shapes every other movement.

Mindful movement is fun, containing at its heart a sense of playfulness, an almost childlike abandon to, and trust of, your body and the sensation of motion. At times it can start to feel like you're floating. It's exciting, new, refreshing, and invigorating each time you engage in the movement. There's a very deep, almost cellular, longing in the body for the creative flow of intelligent energy.

As you begin to follow the flow of energy from your core out into conscious movement, you'll start to notice different qualities of the energy emerging in response to your breathing and the motions your body spontaneously creates. As you begin to trust and rely fully on the natural intelligence of your body-mind, you can surrender completely to a continuously evolving movement, a sense of motion that, over time, will create itself.

The discovery and evolution of mindful movement begins with body awareness. Here lies the essential key for staying attuned to the subtle energies that reside in your body as body memory, and to the more fluid energy of emotions. The more awareness of these body memories and emotions that you can develop, the more you will be able to discharge the accumulated stress of vicarious trauma and re-charge your body and mind with living, intelligent, evolving FlowMotion™.

Emotion arises at the place where mind and body meet. It is the body's reaction to your mind — or you might say a reflection of your mind in the body.

— Eckhart Tolle, *Practicing the Power of Now,* page 24

Body Awareness

How aware are you of your body, both outside and inside? Can you identify a profile outline of your own face? Many people can't. Do you avoid looking at your whole naked body in the mirror? Many people do. When you do look at yourself, do you see your body as it is or how you wish that it was or are afraid that it might be? Do you experience your body as one whole, unified, interdependent system, or as isolated, separate, independent parts and pieces that often seem as though they have a mind of their own? Can you feel yourself on the inside of your body? Do you have a sense of familiarity, comfort, and ease living primarily inside your body? Are you aware of how your body feels inside when you are happy, sad, angry, or peaceful? Where in your body is your awareness welcome and where is it not?

One of the things I like to ask participants in my workshops on Compassion Fatigue is how much time they're actually "present" inside their body, in their here and now reality. Most participants will admit they actually spend very little time inside, fully centered and present in their bodies; they have to admit they're often fantasizing, daydreaming, or caught up in intellectual discussion in their heads. Most participants will guess they probably spend no more than 5 to 10 percent of their time fully present in their bodies.

The next logical question then is "why?" Why do you spend so little time with your awareness present in your body reality? Why is your body awareness usually so connected to your head or face, but so rarely to the rest of you, particularly inside, such as in the heart and guts. If you really were aware, comfortable, and at ease with your body, isn't that where your awareness would want to be?

One of the largest areas of "blindness" for many people is their body-awareness connection, the complete, fully conscious, waking connection to the senses, to the feeling of being a whole, unified, interdependent physical person. The fact that so few people are really body aware is most likely a sign of our collective cultural shame. In our culture you're trained from very young not to be curious and in touch with your body. Simply to touch your body in some places is often met with a sense of guilt and shame. To be fully present, inside your body with all of its sensations and feelings, can require a radical acceptance of yourself in the face of collective guilt.

Body Awareness Exercise #1

Give the following exercise a try. Go into it with the intent to be aware of where your unawareness is. This is a difficult thing to do and requires much self-honesty, but try to be as open, aware, and truthful to your experience as possible, even if it's not what you expected.

Allow yourself the freedom of creative imagination. Imagine that your physical body can become the mirror image of an emotional freeze response. What would it look like if you stood up and took a pose that mirrored this freezing? Would it be tense or relaxed? Where in your body would the tension be? What does it look like to be frozen in motion? Where would your hands and arms be? Would your neck and shoulders be tight and stiff? What would your breathing be like?

Stand up for a moment and try this. Allow your body to take the shape, form, tenseness, and intensity of an emotional freeze response. Feel the sensations associated with emotionally freezing by imagining how you felt the last time you got emotionally or mentally blindsided by a situation that you didn't expect. As you let the jolting of the experience manifest consciously in your body, what do you notice? How do you experience the initial shock? Do you feel emotional electricity? Is there almost a sense of impact as the shock hits you? Do you feel "knocked off balance" for a second?

How does your body respond to such a shock? Are your legs frozen stiff, knees locked? Is your stomach cramped or tense? Do you feel that your breath is frozen, with tension bearing down on your diaphragm, making you unable to breathe out? Are your shoulders held in tight and high toward your ears? Are your arms flexed and held in front with hands out? Is your mouth held open or closed, jaw clenched? Are your eyes wide open and fixed?

Remain in this position for a few seconds. Be sure to hold your breath in and bear down on your diaphragm as though you wanted to scream but can't get the sound out. As much as you are able, allow your awareness to absorb this experience without thinking about it. Just notice and observe without analyzing

What did you find out? Did you get a physical, in-your-body experience of an emotional freeze response? Can you begin to sense the immediate and profound interconnection between mind and body? Could you feel, for even just a second, how alive your body is with emotion and intelligence? Can you imagine how your body can have a memory, even an intelligence of its own that's often not directly connected with your conscious awareness?

Vicarious Trauma and Body Memory

Imagine that your body actually goes through a subtle, less exaggerated version of the above exercise multiple times every day just outside your conscious awareness. There are repeated little jolts, shocks, moments "frozen in time." When you begin to spend more time present in your body, you may be surprised at the number of times you take a "body blow" to the heart or gut from the repeated exposure to trauma and terror that your mind may have already turned off by now.

This is key: vicarious trauma happens in the body. Even though your conscious awareness may not be paying attention to the experience of secondary trauma, your body is continually experiencing (re-)exposure to traumatic stress.

Taken together with our culture's shame of the body and adoration of the brain and intellect, we've become unbalanced in our perception of ourselves. We sometimes come to believe that we are the images we hold in our heads, ignoring the physical reality of the stress and trauma that has accumulated in the body until our physical selves lash out and force us to do so.

As I mentioned earlier, I like to ask participants in my Compassion Fatigue workshops what percentage of time they believe they spend focused in their here and now reality rather than mentally vacationing in Hawaii. Their responses are consistently around 5 to 10 percent. I then ask what percentage of the time their bodies are present. After a moment, the smile of recognition usually appears. Your body is always present in the here and now physical reality. What's closer to the truth from my perspective is that you (your body-mind-self) are continually interacting with numerous energies and forces, seen and unseen, every day. From the moment you open your eyes in the morning, possibly even before then, your body awareness begins to take in and process energy and information. You begin to sense the world with your body as much as you negotiate it with your intellect.

If you were to spend a day from the perspective of your body, what would your experience be like? What would it be like to feel the impact of the repeated jolting your body takes from the continual bombardment of sensations in the world?

Body Awareness Exercise #2

This next exercise requires the help of a partner. It's designed to give your body the awareness and insight it needs to recognize the multiple emotional impacts it receives every day. This recognition can feel like being assaulted by multiple, invisible attackers.

Begin this exercise by taking a body position similar to the one described in the previous exercise. Stand with frozen legs and locked knees. Freeze your stomach, back, shoulders, and neck, holding your breath in and bearing down on your diaphragm. This time hold both hands out in front of you as though you were shouting "Stop!" Your elbows are locked and arms frozen stiff with tension. Close your eyes and begin to count backwards from 100

by sevens, so that you would start with 100, then 93, and so on. As you begin counting, have your partner, without warning, "jolt" your body by firmly tapping one of your outstretched hands on the palm. Your partner should tap just hard enough to send a small shock wave through the frozen arm into your body. If this caused you to lose your place in counting backwards, start over from the beginning.

Continue to keep your body tense and frozen and to restrict the flow of your breath as the exercise continues. Have your partner randomly vary the speed, force, rate, and rhythm of the jolts as you continue to count. Continue the exercise for up to three minutes. If at any point in this exercise you become overly emotional, confused, or disoriented, stop and discontinue.

What was your experience? If you're keeping a journal, a highly recommended activity, take a few minutes to describe your impressions. Many people who have done this exercise in my seminars experience an immediate sensation of being overwhelmed and overloaded with sensory perceptions and not at all prepared for how traumatic even minor, continual, unpredictable jolts to their body-mind system can be. They describe the unpredictability of the jolt as being the most difficult aspect to contend with. As a result, they find themselves constantly tense, even frozen physically, in an attempt to prepare for the next jolt. Some participants describe feeling vulnerable, even frightened, after the first jolt.

It's my belief that this exercise is no more traumatic than experiencing the continual barrage of unpredictable jolts that your body-mind receives daily in ever greater amounts and intensities. Becoming continually distracted, internally preoccupied, and physically numb to the sensations that are continually present in your body does not make them go away or reduce their cumulative risk, over time, to your physical health and emotional well being.

Discharging and Re-charging Energy in MOTION

As we begin the healing process we use what is known as the "felt sense," or internal body sensations. These sensations serve as a portal through which we find the symptoms or reflections of trauma. In directing our attention to these internal body sensations, rather than attacking the trauma head-on, we can unbind and free the energies that have been held in check.

— Peter Levine, Ph.D., *Waking the Tiger: Healing Trauma*, page 66

Continual exposure and re-exposure to the images, sounds, and emotions associated with trauma and terror, particularly when you leave yourself open to unconsciously absorbing this trauma (due to a lack of body awareness), can result in an accumulation of old, stagnant, and frozen *Energy in MOTION*. This residual energy does not simply go away. In fact, it tends to accumulate more experiences that have an energy signature similar to its own.

Every emotion resonates at its own frequency. When memory traces are laid down as body memory, the images, sounds, smells, behaviors, and body sensations of a traumatic experience become encoded with the frequency of the emotion that's experienced. The more traumatic the experience, the greater the force and energy of the emotion generated.

Over time, and with continual re-exposure to situations that remind the body's mind of previous traumatic experiences, an accumulation of residual energy is built up that requires more and more resources to keep it corralled. The more energy corralled, the more resources are required to keep it compartmentalized and separated from your central awareness.

Mindful movement begins with consciously discharging the accumulated, residual energy that's stored in the very muscles, nerves, and tissues of your body by utilizing your "felt sense" or internal body awareness. By guiding your awareness into your body and sensing areas of tension and blocked or frozen energy, you're able to identify where your body's residual energy is corralled.

Take a moment right after you read this to try this exercise. Close your eyes and allow your breath to deepen and slow down. Begin to breathe from your diaphragm. Allow your abdomen to open up as you breathe in to a count of four. Allow the energy of your breath to draw your conscious awareness into your body as you breathe in. As you breathe out to a count of six, breathe your awareness through, in, and around your entire body. Without judging, just allow your sense impressions to enter your awareness. Trust your intuitive consciousness.

Where in your body are you holding onto old, stagnant, frozen energy? Where can you feel the accumulation of stress, strain, and tension that has caused your muscles to freeze with chronic stress? If you're like the majority of participants in my workshops on Compassion Fatigue, you will immediately point to your neck, shoulders, upper back, and the muscles that connect the neck and shoulders. While there are many other places in the body where we hold stress and trauma, these areas seem readily identifiable to most people.

Begin by allowing your conscious awareness to focus specifically on the areas described. Just let your awareness be present in that part of your body. What do you notice? Can you feel areas of tension, soreness, even numbness? What does the body sensation actually feel like? Can you sense any emotional energy intertwined with the physical, bodily sensation? What kind of emotion is it?

Slowly begin to pull your shoulders up and in toward your ears as you inhale. What do you notice? Can you feel tension in the muscles that connect your shoulders and neck as you pull your shoulders up and in? What images come to mind as you sit with your shoulders pulled up to your ears? How does this body position affect your emotions, your sense of self? Notice how you're breathing at this moment. Are you holding your breath in?

Now rotate your shoulders back and down. As you let your shoulders ease down, slowly exhale through your nose in harmony with your movements. Be as conscious as you can of the transitioning of body movement and sensations as you bring your shoulders back with the releasing of your breath. How does this movement make you feel? Can you feel a contrast with the first movement? What sensations or emotions are triggered by this movement?

Repeat the movement. As you breathe in from your diaphragm to a count of four, pull your shoulders up and in toward your ears. Continue breathing to a count of six as you rotate your shoulders up, in, and back by extending your chest and arching your back. As your in-breath transitions to out-breath, allow your shoulders to sink slowly and easily back to their original positions to a count of four.

Allow each part of the movement to be an extension of your breath and awareness. Breathe movement and awareness into your neck and shoulders. Allow your awareness to sink into the muscles and tissues with each motion. Sense the physical tension and "frozen" emotional energy that is locked into the tissues of your muscles, nerves, and tendons.

This time repeat the motion with dynamic tension. Dynamic tension is moving tension. It's a very useful technique because it can enliven, energize, and "un-freeze" old, stagnant energy that has taken root as a freezing numbness within the muscle itself. By tensing, moving, and releasing certain muscles, and connecting tendons in harmony with deep, powerful breaths, you can begin to unbind, free, and discharge some of the residual energy that has taken root in your body.

To begin this exercise, focus your attention on the muscles of your neck and shoulders, particularly the ones that feel tense, frozen, or numb. Allow your attention to imaginatively enter into the muscle itself. Consciously squeeze these muscles as though you were paralyzed by fear. Squeeze using as much tension as you are comfortable with and hold that position as though you were frozen.

How does it feel to consciously freeze a part of your body that typically holds a great deal of your stress? Can you surround that part with your awareness? Where in your neck and shoulders is your awareness able to go freely and where is it not? As you continue to hold this position, what feelings and emotions do you sense? Can you sense the connection and interaction between physical tension and emotional stress?

Now draw in a deep, powerful breath from your diaphragm. Simultaneously pull your shoulders up and in toward your ears to a count of three, using as much tension as you are comfortable with. Rotate your shoulders back to a count of three while arching your back and extending your chest. Hold this position for two seconds,

and then allow your chest and shoulders to slowly collapse inwards as you release your breath, counting to four. Exhale all of your spent oxygen by pushing your breath all out until you feel completely empty.

Repeat the movement again. As you breathe and move, place your awareness into the sensation of moving frozen muscle in harmony with your breath. Allow the tension in your muscles to draw your attention into the muscle tissue itself. Visualize and sense in the muscle tissue the years of frozen, stagnant stress-energy being stimulated, massaged, loosened, enlivened, uprooted, and circulated with your breath, energy, and awareness. Allow your energy and movement to stimulate and circulate the stagnant energy with the flow of your breath, attention, energy, and motion. As you exhale, allow your shoulders and chest to cave inward with a sense of release and relief. Imagine, visualize, and sense the anxiety, fear, panic, stress, helplessness, and all of the other emotions and sensations associated with trauma and terror being released as you release your breath and again become empty.

Try the motion again. This time, allow your attention to focus consciously on every part of each motion. Tense your neck, shoulders, and the muscles that connect them, becoming aware of any little movement that the conscious tension in your muscles may cause. Can you feel a type of shaking or vibrating as you squeeze your neck muscles? Allow your attention to enter into the vibrating muscle. What do you notice? What does the shaking that comes from tensing the muscle remind you of? If the shaking muscle could talk, what would it say?

Allow the vibrating tension to spread from your neck into your shoulders and the muscles that connect them. As you consciously tighten these muscles and place your awareness inside them, what do you notice now? What was the sensation of spreading the tension from your neck to your shoulders? As you squeeze a little harder on these muscles what happens to the rest of your body, your face, arms, hands, and stomach. How are you breathing? What do this body posture, feeling, and tension remind you of? What emotions, thoughts or memories are associated with your body sense right now?

As you begin to breathe in with a powerful, deep breath, slowly pull your shoulders up and in toward your ears, keeping as much tension in the muscle as you're comfortable with. Place your awareness in the muscle as it moves. Imagine that there are actually images, memories, emotions, and sensations stored in the muscle itself that are being released, as though the muscle tension is digging out embedded, stagnant energy that had taken root as chronic, numbing stress and tension.

As you rotate your shoulders back with continuing tension, extend your chest and arch your back. Allow your attention to focus on the transition of body position, from shoulders raised and chest caved in, to shoulders back, chest extended, and back arched. What do you notice? If your body could comment on what it felt like moving from a collapsed position to an extended position, what would it say? Which position is more natural to your body?

Finally, direct your conscious awareness to all of the movement and motions of your whole upper body, your body as one unit, while you release the tension and slowly exhale your breath fully, allowing your neck, shoulders, back, chest, and abdomen to soften, relax, and slowly implode in harmony with your breath. Allow your breath to empty completely as your shoulders relax forward, forming a concave space around your heart.

What is your sense of discharging, letting go, even surrendering the frozen energy that has been locked into your neck and shoulders? Can you glimpse a physical and emotional sense of surrender as the last of your breath is discharged? Will you allow the disengagement and discharging of old, stagnant, *Energy in MOTION?*

Experiment with this movement. Try rotating your shoulders at different speeds and tension levels, varying the tempo and rhythm, or even move your shoulders in reverse. Try breathing with a wide array of lengths, speeds, and intensities.

Begin to focus your attention inward and listen to your own natural rhythm. In aligning breath, motion, movement, and energy with conscious awareness and intent, you'll begin to experience a sense of increased physical, mental, and emotional coherence. Allow your body spontaneous expression of the *Energy in MOTION* that has been corralled as the energy residue of cumulative stress and trauma.

Body Awareness Exercise #3

When you've attained a sense of flow in your movement with the above exercise try adding another element. Begin this exercise seated in a comfortable chair, back straight, with your head hung forward and your neck bent to the extent that it's comfortable. Allow your head to hang without forcing it down. If you're able, rest your chin on your breastplate, shoulders caved in.

Slowly tighten your neck muscles and allow that tension to cause a small shaking in your neck that then travels to your shoulders. As you begin to inhale powerfully and deeply from your diaphragm, begin to raise your neck with continuing tension, in harmony with your shoulders, to a count of four.

Be very careful not to apply too much tension as you move your neck. Your neck may already be very tight from years of freezing emotion. At first apply just gentle pressure, then allow your awareness to enter into your neck muscles as they move. Notice if there's any "cracking."

As you pull your shoulders up and then back, follow the motion with your head, so that it's cocked back as far as it can comfortably go. Point your eyes upwards just as your shoulders are pulled all the way back. Move your chest out and arch your back. Be sure to be very careful and mindful of this motion as your neck bends backwards, remembering not to push or strain the muscles. Apply only gentle pressure, just enough to feel the muscle. Allow your awareness to enter into the muscle itself as you move.

As your in-breath transitions to out-breath, slowly release the tension in your muscles. Feel the pleasure of an exquisite release of stress as your neck slowly bends forward and down in harmony with your shoulders, with your chest collapsing in as you discharge all of your spent oxygen in a long, slow Breath of Relief.

Continue to experiment with this motion. The time will surely be well-spent. In addition to discharging accumulated stress, you're beginning to develop body awareness and body consciousness. Each minute you can spend more fully present inside your body, the more your body awareness grows. You'll be able to notice more quickly when your body becomes tense and when you freeze your breath. You'll also be able to discharge the energy rather than freeze it.

Coordinating conscious breathing and mindful movement to release and discharge corralled, residual energy is one method of discharging *Energy* in *MOTION*. There is a second, somewhat different method that will be discussed and illustrated later in the book that utilizes a type of involuntary trembling that's more connected with "core" trauma and energy.

Breath of Relief and the exercises in the following chapters are specific, easy, energy discharging and renewing movements that can be done literally anywhere. Most people in my workshops who allow themselves fully to engage, physically, emotionally, and mentally in the exercise are able to immediately sense relief and renewal. Breath of Relief and FlowMotion™, practiced regularly, can become vital, positive, re-energizing rituals.

Re-charging

Recent writings about energy and fitness indicate that highly energetic people have different routines or rituals that they use to re-charge their internal stores. Re-charging your energy begins with developing a highly specific routine for managing that energy.

Participants in my Compassion Fatigue workshops are always a little amazed when they really, honestly think about how much time they actually spend consciously, specifically re-charging their energy throughout the day. Most will have to admit that even when there is time available, they're often busy with something that's not nearly as important as self-renewal. Very few people really consider the fact that they actually, physically need to take short breaks throughout the day, just to discharge the daily accumulation of energy residue and re-charge with fresh, new energy. The majority of the fatigue we feel during the day is the result of an energy build-up that's caught or stuck, rather than an actual lack of energy. We get burned up as much as we can get burned out.

So how can we develop these rituals or routines? Do you have any routines that you currently use to manage your energy? What would such a routine look like? How would it work? How long would it take to do? Would you need any special equipment? What would be necessary for a routine to be effective? How would you feel afterwards?

Can you imagine having a specific energy management routine involving conscious breathing and mindful movement that would be simple and easy, would take between 5 and 15 minutes to do, and could be done virtually anywhere? Would you do it?

Chapter Seven:

Breath of Relief

Letting go is a basic, if not *the* basic principle of
T'ai-chi-Ch'uan. It is said a student's progress is
determined by how much he is willing to let go
of — tension, emotional programming, fear, thinking,
defensiveness, etc. The natural being is already
powerful and wise. You must let go of your
interference with the body's power and wisdom.

— Bob Klein, *Movements of Magic*, pages 13-14

Introduction

Breath of Relief and the following exercises that combine together to form FlowMotion™ are the synthesis of conscious breathing and mindful movement. When you're able to consciously breathe energy and awareness into spontaneous, flowing motion that's directed by your felt sense into, through, and around your body-mind for the enjoyment and mastery of the movement, then you're doing FlowMotion™.

Breath of Relief is one whole, separate movement that is at the same time part of and interdependent upon the larger movement that is FlowMotion™. Breath of Relief builds upon the exercises explained in the previous chapters; all of the previous exercises are done to begin developing your body awareness by enlivening your body with conscious breathing and mindful movement. In the same way, Breath of Relief and the following three breathing exercises, Breath of Awareness, Breath of Acceptance, and Breath of Transformation will prepare you physically and energetically for FlowMotion™.

These next four chapters will focus on the conscious breathing and mindful movement that's specific to each of the individual breathing movements: relief, awareness, acceptance, and transformation. As you can tell from the names of the movements, each one is designed to enliven, connect, and harmonize body and mind by connecting breath, awareness, energy, and motion in different body positions and alignments.

Each chapter will describe the structure and process of each exercise including the stance, breath, motion, and visualization. Each movement has its own self-organizing function that nurtures spontaneous expression and evolution.

Next, some ideas on how to practice the movement will be offered. Knowing the movement and doing the movement are sometimes two different realities. Breath of Relief is a very simple, easy to do exercise. Its simplicity can be deceiving. We can sometimes almost unconsciously attribute effectiveness to effort and complexity. Breath of Relief is neither; its power is its simplicity.

Breath of Relief is meant to be simple and easy to do. When many people visualize themselves "exercising" they often establish a picture of forcing themselves with great effort to exercise strenuously with little or no enjoyment. Exercise is often seen as a "necessary evil," most often avoided because it's automatically perceived as something that you *have* to do rather than an activity you look forward to doing, in fact will crave to do, once your body attunes itself to your own natural flow and rhythm.

Breath of Relief is easy to do, easy to get started, takes a minimal amount of initial commitment, and gives you an immediate pay-back. As soon as you allow yourself the freedom to enter into a type of awareness you rarely remember experiencing, you'll sense an immediate, highly enjoyable flow of energy and awareness in, around, and through your body and mind.

What's most important to remember about practicing Breath of Relief is that you should do it for the enjoyment of the experience. It's not designed to help you lose weight, enhance your appearance, or prepare you to run a marathon; it's designed to give your body an immediate feeling of aliveness and awareness. When you practice Breath of Relief engage in each motion with the same open curiosity you had as a child. Take each movement for what it is. The benefit is in the intrinsic, in-your-body enjoyment of doing of the movement, not in getting finished with it.

The Stance

The earth is calling to you. It has something for you. This great creature upon which we live wishes to give you its energy to empower your life.

— Bob Klein, *Movements of Magic,* page 8

One of your major "energy-arteries" travels up from the earth, through the bottom of your feet, and into your knees and legs. The way in which you stand has everything to do with how aware and receptive you are to one of your greatest sources of energy, the earth.

Although your feet are actually very sensitive you often don't have much awareness in them. This is because most of us experience the center or locus of our awareness in our heads, where the ego lives. The greater the stress level, the louder the ego gets, demanding ever greater amounts of energy and attention to its personal urgent agenda.

How you stand on your feet is very often a good reflection of how you stand in your life. Take a moment and stand up; just notice how you stand. How does it feel to "be in your shoes?" What's your balance like? Do you lean to one side or another? How steady do you feel on your feet? Does your weight shift from one foot to the other? How centered in your body do you feel? Where is the "weight" or center of gravity in your body? Can you feel yourself connected to the ground?

Now try standing with your feet a bit wider than shoulder width apart, knees slightly bent, back straight, toes pointing out just slightly to the left and right. Pretend that you're riding an imaginary horse; in most karate styles this stance is actually called the Horse Stance.

Hold your hands in front of you as though you were holding a large beach ball out from your body. Your hands should be about 18 inches apart from each other, elbows slightly bent, and palms facing toward each other and slightly down. Allow your arms and shoulders to relax. Relax your neck, straighten your back, and imaginatively allow your core center to drop down just a little; let your core "float."

Focus your attention on your feet and *in* your feet. Can you do it? Can you get your attention to travel from your head all the way down to your feet? If you're having difficulty feeling your feet, slightly curl your toes inward and then outward, pressing down on your feet, until you can feel a sense of aliveness in your soles.

Use your creative imagination and place your awareness in your feet. Imagine that you're looking up at yourself from the point of view of your feet. What do you look like? How would your feet recognize you? What would your opinion of yourself be from that vantage point? What kind of relationship do you believe your feet have with you? Be honest: how do you treat your feet?

Now direct your attention to the ground and *into* the ground. What's your relationship with the earth, with gravity? Ever thought

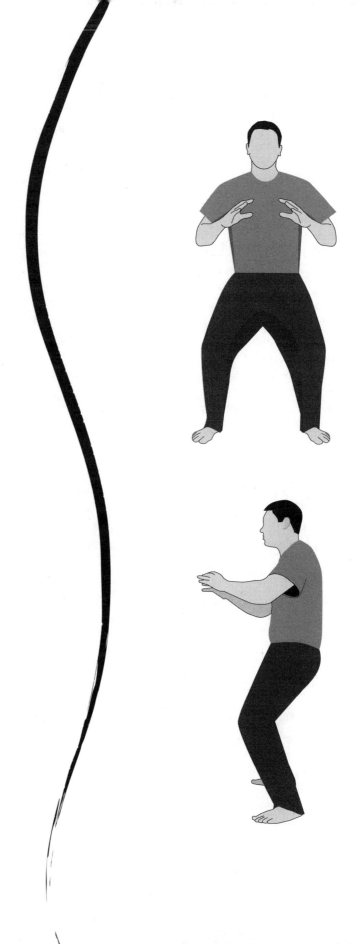

about it? Each of us has a very unique, individual, and intimate relationship between our feet, gravity, and the ground. As a professional speaker who's on his feet most of the day, I've become acutely aware, at times painfully, of that relationship.

Allow your awareness to expand to include sensing the energy that's literally absorbed into, and radiating out from, the earth. Sense your personal connection with the earth and with this energy. Do you experience yourself as a part of, even an extension of, this living earth upon which we live? Or do you feel disconnected from this enormous energy source?

Consciously engage your creative imagination to extend and attune your awareness to sense the living, flowing energy that constantly radiates up from the earth. Visualize and imaginatively sense this energy penetrate the soles of your feet and extend through your knees and thighs to your core. Can you feel this connection to the energy of the earth? Can you sense that this connection is two-way? What might the earth be absorbing from your core energy?

When your feet are grounded, when they feel solidly connected to the earth's surface, allow your awareness to travel upwards to your ankles and knees. Just place your awareness there, both inside and outside. What do you notice? How strong or fragile do you feel in these two connecting, bending, rotating body parts? Do you suffer from ongoing soreness, stiffness, or swelling? How does that affect your sense of connection with the ground and with the energy that's moving up and down the "inside" of your legs?

Ankles, legs, and knees (especially the knees) are often considered areas of potential weakness and vulnerability (weak in the knees, don't have a leg to stand on). In Muay Thai, a type of kickboxing, legs and knees are considered prime targets because of their vulnerability to attack, and once the legs go a person can't continue fighting. The same is true in terms of the mind-body. Much of the *base* of our sense of self can actually be felt in the legs and knees. The feeling-sense of being grounded *in* reality has its physical existence in your legs and your awareness of being in your legs.

One of the quickest, most effective ways to ground yourself, to bring yourself back from an emotional hijacking, is to firmly squeeze your calves and thighs while fully and consciously discharging your breath with a sigh of relief. This will return your attention to your legs and feet and with being connected to the ground.

As you stand with your back straight and knees slightly bent, how do you feel? Gently bounce your weight up and down by flexing and relaxing your knees (if you are having problems with your knees, be very gentle and consult your healthcare provider before trying anything that may cause you pain or injury). As you bounce your weight up and down, imagine there's a fluid, plasma-like energy in your core that bounces along with your motion. As you bounce down allow your center of gravity to fall by relaxing your legs and letting gravity carry your weight down. Just as you reach the bottom of the bounce, begin to flex the muscles in your legs to stop the downward motion.

At the transition point between falling and bouncing up notice how this fluid, plasma energy in your core continues to flow down, all the way through your knees out the bottoms of your feet, and into the ground. As you begin to flex your knees and legs to start the upward motion, sense that you're drawing up your core energy from the earth. Continue to bounce up, feeling the momentum of your core energy as it reaches a natural apex, then begin the downward motion again. Bounce in this way several times. Engage your conscious breathing and creative imagination to extend your breath with your core energy by sharply discharging your breath "into the ground" as you bounce down.

How does the energy feel? Does it pass cleanly from your core through your legs, knees, ankles, and feet, or are there places where your awareness of the energy does not go? Can you feel yourself on the inside? Are you present in your feet, ankles, knees and legs? Now let your attention just rest in your core. When you allow your awareness to imaginatively enter into this symbolic center of your body-mind, what do you notice (besides your stomach growling)? As stated previously, one of the most important, yet energetically under-nourished energy centers in your body-mind is your core, and the more you can feel and "feed" your core with nourishing energy, the more stable, whole, and coherent your sense of self.

Bring your attention up now to the center of your body, your pelvis, the small of your back, your abdomen, diaphragm, chest, and heart, to the heart of your being. How does your awareness feel in this part of your body? How alive and vibrant do you feel internally? Can you feel your heart? Can you feel yourself inside your heart? What kind of relationship do you have with your heart? Place your attention in the part of your chest that energetically feels

to be your emotional heart center; this may be different than the location of your actual physical heart. Let your intuition and sensitivity be your guides. Can you sense a vortex of aware, intelligent, energy? Can you feel a presence? Can you imagine your heart as feeling and intelligent? Can you feel yourself inside your heart? Is your heart "light" or "heavy?" Have you experienced a broken heart, possibly a shattered one? How much energy is flowing through your heart center? What kind of energy is it? Is it flowing or freezing?

Now allow the awareness that's in your heart center to extend downward to your core. As you breathe in, imagine a flow of energy and information from your core extending with your breath to your heart. As you breathe out, visualize energy from your heart extending to your core. Imagine this energy-information super-highway also extending upward from your heart to your head and brain.

Allow your awareness now to travel up and down what may be visualized as an intelligent, living, energy-information conduit that flows up and down the center of your body, from the top of your head, through your legs, and out the bottoms of your feet into the ground. As you breathe in and out, sense the energy flowing from

the ground, up through your legs, to the core into your heart, and out the top of your head with the in-breath, and then back down the same path as you exhale. Allow your awareness to flow freely with your breath, energy, and motion. What do you notice? Can you sense, feel and visualize this vibrant, living, flowing *Energy* in *MOTION?*

Now allow your awareness to feel the structure and support of your back and your spine, particularly your lower back. Place your attention into your lower back as you continue to breathe energy through your core. What do you notice?

The lower back is often a point of soreness with many people because of the accumulation of undischarged, residual freeze energy. Each time your body goes into an unconscious, involuntary freeze response your lower back also freezes. The accumulation of freeze-energy there can result in chronic tightness, soreness, and inflexibility, creating a literal pain in the neck.

As you focus your attention on your lower back, allow your awareness to surround and penetrate any tightness or soreness. Breathe your awareness into your lower back and just observe, sense, and feel the tight soreness. What do you notice? How would you describe the sensations? If your lower back could talk, how would it describe the tight soreness? Would there be any emotion in your lower back's voice? Which emotion?

Bring your attention to your hands, arms, shoulders, and neck. Can you get a sense of energy in your hands, arms and shoulders from holding them out? Are you tense in your neck and shoulders? Breathe a deep breath and consciously relax your shoulders by letting them drop as your exhale. Allow your shoulders gently to roll slightly forward.

Direct your attention to your hands. Place your awareness in the palms of your hands. Do you feel anything, a tingling or warmth? Right in the center of your palms is an area about the size of a silver dollar that's very sensitive to energy. Can you feel it? At times you may notice a sense of pressure or even a vacuum-like sensation that seems to connect with and draw energy in. Other times, your palms may get warm and feel like they're radiating energy. When you're emotionally attuned to somebody you can often feel their emotional energy in your palms.

If you're reading this book for the second time and want to see how the exercises look when they're actually, physically done, please put the DVD that came with the book into your player now. It starts with this first exercise.

Readjust your position so that you feel comfortable and relaxed. Your feet should be wider than shoulder width apart, knees slightly bent, back straight, and toes pointing out just slightly to the left and right. Hold your hands in front of you as though you were holding a large beach ball out from your body, elbows slightly bent, palms facing down. Allow your arms and shoulders to relax. Relax your neck and straighten your back as you allow your center to float.

As you draw a long, slow, deep breath from your diaphragm, allow your breath to pull energy and awareness from the earth, through the bottoms of your feet, and into your core. As fresh oxygen expands your abdomen, observe your awareness as it radiates outward from your core, circulating through, and connecting to, every part of your body. As you slowly exhale gently pushing all of the oxygen out of your lungs, allow your energy and awareness to contract back through your core, into your legs, and out the bottoms of your feet into the earth, moving back out through the same conduit through which it came in.

Using this exercise, you can begin to become more body aware, more knowledgeable about what goes on inside your own skin.

Breath and Motion

Breath and motion have an intimate relationship; you tend to move with the same force, fluidity, and connectedness as you breathe. When you're anxious and breathing in short, shallow, uneven breaths, your movements will also tend to be jerky and uneven. When you consciously breathe smooth, flowing, and connected breaths, your motion is also more likely to be smooth, flowing, and connected.

For this next exercise, continue in the same position as before, with your arms extended, elbows bent, and your hands held in front of you. As you take a long, deep in-breathe through your nose, slowly, gently and smoothly pull your hands and arms toward you.

This time, instead of drawing breath and energy from the earth through your feet, visualize that you're drawing energy in through your palms. Engage your creative imagination to sense the energy that is being pulled in. Can you feel it? Focus your attention on a circle the size of a silver dollar in the middle of both palms. As your hands are breathed in toward your heart, sense the feeling of an opening in the palms that is "drinking in" living, nourishing energy from the environment around you. The soles of your feet aren't the only places in your body that absorb, navigate, discharge, and transmute Energy in *MOTION*. Your palms can be engaged as well.

Because these parts of your body can engage directly with the external world, it can be more beneficial for the exchange of energy to practice Breath of Relief in a natural environment with plants, trees, or water. Mountains and certain geographical formations can conduct large energies as well. If you're in an office, have an inspiring picture of the ocean, mountains, or other natural energy vortices to focus on. If you're allowed, have living plants and running water, like from a small fountain, in your office. It's also good to have happy pictures and certain positive power objects to help conduct and transmute Energy in *MOTION*.

Coordinate your breath and motion so that your hands are being pulled in to your chest as far as they can comfortably go just as you are breathing in as much as you can without strain. Now effortlessly and seamlessly allow the momentum of your in-breath and motion to transition into out-breath and motion.

Just as your in-breath transforms to out-breath, allow the momentum of your pulling-in motion smoothly and seamlessly to transition into an outward pushing motion. In the same way, allow the motion of your breath to smoothly and seamlessly transition from in-breath to out-breath.

As you slowly let your breath out from your mouth to a count of six, mirror your breath with your motion as your hands flow out with your breath. Sense the energy, awareness and intelligence in your hands.

Exhale breath awareness energy *into* your hands as they begin to flow back to their original position. As you slowly release your breath while your arms effortlessly extend forward, focus your attention on and into the silver dollar spot in your palms.

Utilize your creative imagination to feel, sense, and visualize energy pouring out of your palms as you exhale. It's as if your breath is actually pushing the energy out through the silver dollar spot in your palms: the more intensely you exhale your breath, the greater the volume of energy pushed out.

Try the movement again. As you slowly, consciously, pull in a slow, deep, even breath from your diaphragm to a count of four, allow your hands and arms to mirror your breath. As lightly, smoothly, and fluidly as you can, pull your hands in toward your heart in harmony and coordination with your breath.

As you pull your hands toward your chest, feel a vibrant, nurturing energy being pulled with your palms into your heart center. As you fill your lungs with fresh oxygen, imagine that you simultaneously fill your heart with fresh vibrant energy; allow this energy to circulate through your heart center. Visualize this living and intelligent *Energy* in *MOTION* freeing old, stagnant freeze-energy that has taken root as body memory.

As in-breath transitions to out-breath, allow your breath to escape slowly, smoothly, and fluidly to a count of six. Simultaneously, allow the momentum of your inward pulling motion to swing into an outward pushing motion. This time push your hands out with just a slight bit of effort as though you were pushing water out in a swimming pool. Feel the wave of momentum and energy as your hands push out old, stagnant freeze-Energy in *MOTION* that has been released from your heart.

Consciously push your breath out of your mouth. As you breathe out, restrict the passage of breath by constricting your throat while saying "Ahhh…" without using your voice. This will cause you to push harder from your diaphragm. Push all of your air out to a count of three.

As you discharge your breath also discharge your energy. Visualize old, tired, frozen energy being discharged with your breath as you simultaneously push freeze energy from your heart center through your palms.

Visualize this energy being discharged from your heart through the energy center in your palms and out into the environment where it immediately bonds with new, fresh, living energy.

Practice this motion several times, slowly, smoothly, and evenly. What's most important to focus on is the coordination of breath, energy, and motion. As you get into a rhythm of breath, energy, and motion, allow your attention to center in your core. With each motion your body is "remembering" the sensation of flow.

Now we will add another vital component to Breath of Relief: pulling energy from the ground through your feet into your core as you breathe in, and discharging your spent breath and energy back into the ground as you exhale. This is done simultaneously as you pull in and discharge energy from your palms.

Begin this movement starting from the original standing position. Focus on your core. This time, gently bend your knees and allow gravity to pull your center slowly toward the ground as you breathe in to a count of four. Breathe energy in from the earth through the soles of your feet, up your ankles and knees, and directly into your core.

At the same time allow your hands to flow in toward your chest, pulling in vital new energy through your palms and into your heart center. Coordinate your movements so that your hands and arms contract toward your heart center as your knees slowly bend to the force of gravity, lowering your center of gravity toward the ground.

Open your core and your heart to living, intelligent, nurturing, and connecting energy as you breathe in fully from your diaphragm. Sense, feel, and visualize this energy being drawn up from the ground, through your feet, and in through your palms as your legs and arms contract in harmony.

Bend your knees and lower your center of gravity only to the degree that you're comfortable. Don't push or strain for results. If you can't bend down very far at first that's completely fine. If you have pain or injury to your back or knees, consult your healthcare provider before doing this exercise.

As you bend your knees and lower your center of gravity pay attention to your back and your balance. Beginners have a tendency to bend forward as they lower their center of gravity, and they consequently lose their alignment. Just follow the pull of gravity, always

trusting the natural pull of the earth as well as the natural motion of your body.

As you bend your knees and lower your center of gravity, hold your back with a little arch so that your pelvis is slightly tilted forward. Allow gravity to do its work; you just supply the brakes. As you slowly bend your knees, keeping a slight arch in your back, allow gravity to slowly, smoothly, and gently pull you toward the ground.

When you reach that place where you can't comfortably bend your legs and knees, allow your center to slow its momentum. Your hands are pulled in toward your chest. Your lungs are filled with fresh oxygen and your core and your heart are charged with energy.

Just as the momentum in your legs begins to shift from down to up, allow your legs to gently, slowly, and smoothly bounce during the space that your in-breath shifts to out-breath. During this point of transition from down to up, in to out, inhale to exhale, there's a sweet moment of weightlessness and timelessness as breath, energy, motion, and momentum meet at the Gate of Emptiness.

As you complete the gentle bounce, begin breathing out as you sense the momentum in your legs pushing you up. As much as you can, "ride" on the momentum created by the downward motion. Convert the downward energy into upward energy by "bouncing" on the ball of energy that has been created by your breath, energy, and motion.

Breathe energy and awareness from your core into your thighs, knees, ankles, and back as you begin to stand. Just as your momentum carries you out of the gentle bounce to standing, visualize you are consciously breathing awareness-energy into the muscles of your thighs, knees, ankles, and back, actually propelling them into a standing position. Use minimal muscle energy to lift your body upwards. Open yourself to a different kind of energy created and directed by breath, energy, and motion. It's the energy of effortless effort.

As you execute the motions above, breathe energy-awareness from your heart center into your hands as your arms begin to straighten effortlessly. Allow this energy-awareness to propel your arms and hands forward with as little consciously directed effort on your part as possible.

Breathe out slowly, smoothly, and continuously to a count of six. Activate your felt-sense and visualize your breath energy releasing old, stagnant freeze-energy from your heart. Imagine this energy being dispelled as you slowly sigh out a deep, resonant, Breath of Relief.

As your legs and arms straighten in harmony with the slow releasing of your breath, allow your attention to rest in your core. From your core, expand your awareness in all directions, so that your attention is instantly and simultaneously connected to the breath, energy, and motion that are in every part of your body.

From hands to feet, elbows to ankles, all parts of the body flow together as one, while retaining their identities as separate individual units. Without any sense of fragmentation, your awareness is able to move fluidly from experiencing your body as separate, individual parts, to experiencing your body as one whole, indivisible unit, to experiencing your body as both, simultaneously.

As your breath empties out completely, and you return to your original starting position, feel the full completion of the movement. Do not rush or try to get finished with it. Allow the movement to complete itself.

Just as the last of your oxygen is being discharged and you're returning to your original starting position, place your attention into your core. Is the earth calling to you again? If you intuitively sense that it is, allow the momentum of your upward motion to seamlessly transition into downward motion as you open your core, heart, and lungs to fresh, new, vital *Energy in MOTION*.

As you slowly, consciously, pull in a slow, deep, even breath from your diaphragm to a count of four, allow your hands and arms to mirror your breath. As lightly, smoothly and fluidly as you can, pull your hands in toward your heart in harmony and coordination with your breath.

Simultaneously, as your diaphragm opens to draw in oxygen, allow your awareness to be in the soles of your feet as you draw energy in from the earth. Draw energy and awareness from the earth through the soles of your feet into your ankles, knees, and thighs.

This time, as you begin to bend your knees, hold just a little tension in your legs as you consciously squeeze your thigh muscles while lowering your center of gravity to the ground. Squeeze just hard enough to feel the muscles move, but don't inhibit the movement.

As you pull your hands toward your chest, feel a vibrant, nurturing energy being pulled with your palms into your heart center. As you fill your lungs with fresh oxygen, imagine that you also fill your heart with fresh vibrant energy; allow this energy to circulate through your heart center. Visualize this living and intelligent *Energy in MOTION* freeing old, stagnant freeze-energy that has taken root as body memory.

As you continue to squeeze your thigh muscles in harmony with your breath and downward motion, bring your attention to your stomach; this is often where you hold old, stagnant freeze-energy. Consciously breathe energy and awareness into your stomach: what do you feel? Can you sense the years of frozen, petrified energy that have accumulated there?

As in-breath transitions to out-breath, allow your breath to escape slowly, smoothly, and fluidly to a count of six. Allow the momentum in your hands that collected from the inward pulling motion to swing them into an outward pushing motion.

This time push your hands out and your legs up, in harmony and with controlled effort as though you were doing Breath of Relief in a swimming pool. Feel the wave of momentum and energy push out old, stagnant freeze-Energy in *MOTION* that has been released from your heart and stomach.

Consciously push your breath out of your mouth, restricting the passage of breath by constricting your throat while saying a silent "Ahhh…." This will cause you to push harder from your diaphragm. Push all of your air out to a count of three.

As you discharge your breath in a sigh of relief, also discharge your energy. Visualize old, tired, frozen energy being pushed out with your breath and through the energy centers in your palms and feet. Now picture this old energy flowing into the air and earth, mixing with fresh energy.

Once again, pause in that sweet moment of suspension, where time, energy, and motion have paused between out-breath and in-breath and listen internally; can you hear the call? Is your Natural Self inviting you to immerse yourself in the free-flowing play of breath and motion?

Practicing Breath of Relief

Breath of Relief is the first and possibly most important breathing movement to learn. It sets the stage for the next three breaths, Awareness, Acceptance, and Transformation. Each of these breathing motions will build upon the foundation established from practicing Breath of Relief.

Watch the DVD several times to get a sense of the flow of one motion into the next. What is most important about Breath of Relief is that you allow yourself to relax, breathe, and get familiar with your body-self. There is no one, single, "correct" way to do Breath of Relief; your correct way will probably look different than my correct way.

What you may want to focus on initially is the smoothness of your motions in harmony with your breathing. This means letting go of the idea that one way of moving is better than another, and allowing your attention to simply focus on moving hands, arms, and legs harmoniously with your breath.

You'll soon develop a rhythm, which is good as long as you don't confine yourself to just one rhythm. Continually maintain responsiveness to your body-mind by being open to whatever speed, tempo, and intensity it wants to move. Learn to suspend the constant talk of the ego by continually returning to the flow of your breath, energy, and motion.

Try varying the speed of the movement and listen for what feels right to you at that time. As you practice Breath of Relief, you'll become attuned to the various, subtle energy patterns and rhythms that flow through your body every day. The right speed one day may not be the right speed the next.

The more you can allow your awareness to flow in, between, and through every motion of Breath of Relief, the more you'll be attuned to the subtle energies that can help you establish your "inner rhythm" for the day.

When you're familiar and comfortable with the movements, focus on your breathing. Experiment with your breath, motion, and awareness. Try doing the movements with varying speeds and intensities in synchronization with the varying speeds and intensities of your breathing.

You can try a short, intense, and powerful breathing pattern and match that pattern with short, intense, and powerful movements. You can control the intensity and power of your movements by controlling how hard and how many muscles you tense, squeeze, and move with dynamic tension. The harder you squeeze your muscles, the shorter and more powerful the breath.

Continually focus on the physical-emotional sense of letting go of old, stagnant, frozen energy that has taken root in your body as body memory. Each time you exhale, engage your full imagination to sense, feel, and visualize your body letting go of both the daily residue of secondary traumatic stress and the energy that may have been trapped in your body for years from traumatic experiences of the past.

Each time you do Breath of Relief is different than the time before. Continually focus on the newness and freshness of each movement each time. When you're able to do the movement for three minutes continuously, smoothly, fluidly with your attention centered and focused, it's time to move to Breath of Awareness.

Chapter Eight:

Breath of Awareness

Awareness and emotion are really just two parts of perception and are closely intertwined. The "frequency" of your emotion has great influence on the quality and direction of your awareness.

Introduction: What is Awareness?

What is awareness? Have you ever thought deeply about it? What does it mean to be aware of something? What's the process of becoming aware of something? Are there different types and levels of awareness? Is awareness automatic or is it selective? Can we be unaware of something, even if it really does exist? Can we be aware of things that don't really exist? Are we always consciously directing our awareness, or does it sometimes seem to direct itself? Can we be aware of something that we don't recognize? Is there such a thing as motivated unawareness? What's the relationship between self-honesty and self-awareness?

As a trauma survivor-therapist, I've struggled deeply and intensely with the concept of awareness and ways to increase my self-awareness. One of the things I've learned from my struggles is that stress and Compassion Fatigue confine and compartmentalize your awareness. In essence, the more that stress and Compassion Fatigue have challenged or weakened your sense of self-cohesion, the more confined and compartmentalized your awareness is likely to be.

The residual frozen energy that accumulates as Compassion Fatigue contains emotionally charged memory fragments that are actually "pieces" of awareness that have been frozen in time. These pieces of awareness are memory fragments containing images of yourself and others in the experience of traumatic emotional stress. They're still charged with "freeze" energy and will attract and draw other awareness-experiences of a similar emotional charge to them. If the emotional charges from these awareness-experiences are discordant enough with your ego self-image, they'll become confined, isolated and compartmentalized: the more traumatic and discordant the experience, the greater the compartmentalization.

When awareness is compartmentalized it doesn't go inactive. Awareness and emotion are really just two parts of perception and are closely intertwined. The "frequency" of your emotion has great influence on the quality and direction of your awareness.

When the emotion-awareness of a traumatic experience is compartmentalized and stored as body memory it will actively and continually seek expression; this is just the nature of *Energy in MOTION*. In order to prevent the expression and realization of this discordant emotion-awareness, the central ego must continually exert and expend energy to corral and confine it, that is, to actively disown it. As explained before, actively and persistently disowning a portion of your awareness weakens your self-structure because you're splitting yourself into fragments, expending continually increasing amounts of energy to keep those sections split and corralled. The more you reject and disown a part of yourself, the more that part is actually "fed" energy. You're diverting energy from nourishing and consolidating your sense of self to fragmenting and compartmentalizing your self-structure.

In addition, the more you disown a portion of yourself the more autonomy you give it to become increasingly independent of, and non-responsive to, your central self-awareness. The more experiences of a similar emotional charge that register and take root as body memory, the more powerful, independent, and non-responsive these "islands" of emotion-awareness become. In extreme cases, borderline personality disorder and dissociative identity disorder, formerly known as multiple personality, can ensue. When awareness is attached to emotions with a different, more positive frequency, such as care, appreciation, and enjoyment, just the opposite tends to happen; rather than isolation and compartmentalization, there's a merging, a synthesizing, and a consolidation. A cohesion of self emerges.

Awareness is intimately connected with your willingness to be honest with yourself. Self-honesty, self-awareness, and self-acceptance go hand in hand. You'll always be self-aware to the extent you can be self-honest and accepting. Another interesting facet of awareness is its intimate connection with your body. Body tension, position, momentum, and activation are all closely associated with awareness and emotion, as are the rate, flow, and intensity of your breathing. If you really want to become aware of the energy and information that are encoded in body memory, pay very close attention to the moment-to-moment presence within your body-mind, especially your rate and flow of breathing when you enter into different emotional states throughout the day. The more you can remain centered in your body, observing the transitioning of emotions in concert with various body tensions, positions, and momentum, the more aware of the subtle energy messages that are encoded into your body memory you will become.

The Stance

To begin Breath of Awareness, take a stance similar to the opening stance for Breath of Relief. Allow your feet to connect to the energy continuously emanating from the earth by standing squarely and fully in your soles. Feel that connection the bottoms of your feet have with the earth. Consciously visualize and sense in your feet and legs that you're absorbing this living, nourishing energy.

Your feet should be a bit wider than shoulder width apart, knees slightly bent, with toes pointing forward as though you were riding a horse. Keep your back straight, rather than leaning forward, to help your core sink and center. You should feel the added pressure in your leg muscles as you slowly raise and lower your center by "bouncing" your Qi as though it were a fluid that flowed through the middle of your body.

When you feel centered and balanced as though your core were floating, slowly begin to reach up with both hands over your head toward the sky. Reach up very slowly as you begin to exhale your breath. Consciously push out your breath by flexing your diaphragm, moving all of the old, residual oxygen and energy from your lungs. Imagine that the atmosphere outside of you is a vacuum and that it's drawing all of this residual material out.

As you exhale from your mouth, allow the air to pass through your vocal chords without activating your voice. Open your throat and mouth and allow the escaping air to be funneled by tightening the muscles of your throat. As you funnel oxygen through your throat with a slight push from the diaphragm, silently say the word "Ahhh…," so that the air rushes through your vocal chords without activating your voice.

Continue to push all of the air from your diaphragm as you reach up, both palms facing toward the sky. With your eyes, follow the raising of your palms, slowly and gently bending your head and neck backwards. As you move your head, place your attention in the muscles at the back of your neck. Allow your awareness to imaginatively enter into the muscle tissue, the tendons, and connecting bone. What do you notice? Can you feel the pressure in the back of your neck as your chin slowly rises? Does it feel tight and brittle? Does your neck make a snapping noise as you continue

to bend it backward? How tight do you feel in your neck? Is there some old, frozen, energy residue that's stored in the muscles and tissues of your neck as body memory? If the back of your neck had a voice and a story to tell, what would it say?

Continue to raise your palms toward the sky as you begin to straighten out your knees and arch your back. As your hands reach as far up as they can go, with still a slight bend in your knees (never completely straighten your knees in any of these exercises), allow your weight and balance to just slightly bend backwards as you push out the last of your breath. Arch your back slowly and gently just until you can feel the small of your back.

As the last of your breath is being discharged, allow your attention to extend from the back of your neck into the small of your back. Extend your awareness by keeping one part of your attention in your neck as it stretches down toward the small of your back. Feel your awareness extend itself as though it were actually traveling through your backbone, connecting back and neck. What could this part of your body tell you if it had a voice? Would it complain about the stress it's been under? Would it say it's been back break-ing, or that the world is on its shoulders? Would it scream for you to "get it off my back?"

The plain and simple truth of it is, your body does talk, and its voice usually consists of pain, distress, tightness, soreness, and fragil-ity, and if it goes unheeded it eventually breaks down, freezes up, and is very unforgiving when you want to move. Your body is a living, intelligent creature all by itself. It's worth listening to.

Breath and Movement

You should now be standing firmly rooted to the ground, your body in alignment, with your knees and elbows slightly bent, reaching toward the sky with your palms facing upward. Your head, neck, and back are all slightly arched, your eyes are focused on your hands, and your lungs are empty. Allow yourself to be completely empty for just a couple of seconds.

As the vacuum of emptiness easily and naturally transforms to the inhalation of breath, allow your outwardly focused energy to

begin to collapse inward. Just as exhaling your breath created a wave of air out away from you that will eventually transform and return to the source, your Qi energy also travels out from you to eventually return.

As you begin to take in a long, slow, deep breath to a count of four from your diaphragm, visualize that you're reaching up into a pool or vortex of pure awareness-energy. Imagine that you're pulling in this awareness-energy through your palms as you begin to draw in your hands. The degree you're able to empty yourself of stagnant, frozen energy is the degree to which you can absorb the living, flowing, and vibrant awareness-energy.

As you continue to draw your hands down toward your center, breathe in slowly and smoothly from your diaphragm. Engage your creative imagination and visualize that your palms are actually drinking in the living, flowing awareness-energy that's being drawn toward your core. Imagine that you're breathing this awareness-energy into every cell in your body.

As you bend your elbows to pull in your hands, also bend your knees and slowly, gently, lower your center of gravity. Be sure to keep your back straight, rather than bending forward, and be care-ful not to strain your back or knees.

Lowering your center of gravity is really an art; it's actually more complex and more central to experiencing your core than you'd think. Lowering your center means allowing the earth to pull you closer to it while the resilience in your legs and knees effortlessly softens the pull of gravity so that you experience a sensation of float-ing gently toward the ground. You're neither in a free-fall, nor con-sciously resisting gravity, rather, you've surrendered your individual ego-will and empowered your body-mind, the Natural Self that lives in your core, to literally hold you up or to ease you down.

As you allow your core to float effortlessly toward the earth, con-tinue to breathe in fully from your diaphragm. Begin to extend and connect your awareness, from your palms pulling and drink-ing in revitalizing energy, to your incoming breath circulating that energy-awareness to your core. As you breathe in, become consciously receptive to the energy and awareness. Allow yourself to feel, and be changed by, the experience of conscious energy-awareness. What kinds of changes would you anticipate by allowing conscious energy-awareness?

As you continue to pull your hands toward your center, notice how they effortlessly rotate inward so that your palms face each other by the time they're eye-level. Be aware of the sensation in the back of your neck as your head moves with your eyes, following your hands. Can you feel the release of tension?

Continue to follow your hands with your eyes as they're pulled down toward your chest and heart by the same energy that floats your center. Your lungs are beginning to feel full with oxygen. Can you sense the accumulation of fresh, vital energy and awareness in your lungs, chest, and particularly your heart? Can you also extend and connect the awareness between your heart and your core?

As your hands continue their downward path, your legs and knees also continue to bend, slowly and smoothly lowering your center of gravity toward the earth to the extent you're comfortable. If you experience unusual pain or tightness in your knees or back, discontinue the exercise and consult your healthcare provider before continuing. As you allow your center of gravity to be pulled closer to the earth, keep your back straight so that you don't bend forward with the motion. Allow the full weight of your body to be supported by your legs and suspended in your center.

As the downward momentum of your physical movement begins to slow and then come to a point of suspension, notice how the momentum of your Qi energy, the fluid, plasma-like energy that runs through the center of your body, continues its downward movement through your knees, ankles, and out the bottom of your feet into the earth. Simultaneously pay attention to how the Qi energy in your palms continues to circulate with the Qi energy that flows with your breath, in, around, and through your heart.

Visualize that you're actually pulling, breathing, and circulating this energy from the top of your head, down the midline of your body, and into your heart. Continue to visualize this energy connecting and circulating between your heart and your core, your core and the earth. With a single, fluid motion of your hands, in synergy with your breath and the motion of your body, you're drawing in and circulating vital awareness energy through your entire body.

Just as your hands flow down to heart level, palms facing each other, allow your elbows to flair out, increasing the distance between your palms as well as opening and expanding your chest and lungs. Continue to follow your hands with your eyes, bending

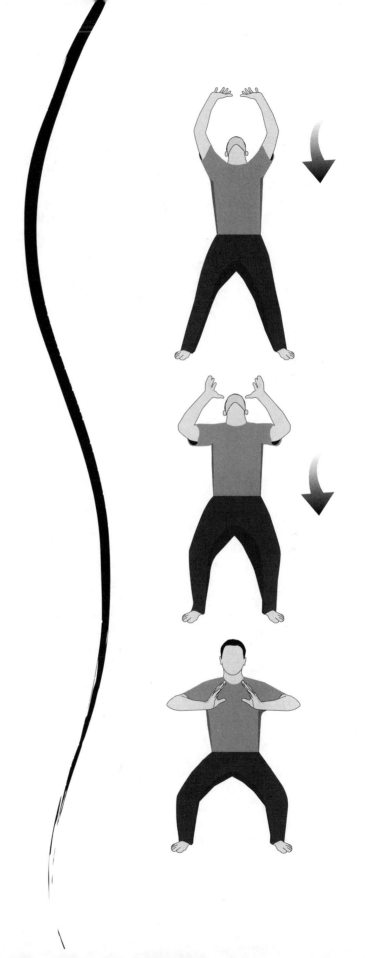

your head and neck down and forward as your hands reach heart level. Can you release the tightness in your neck as it bends gently forward?

As the momentum in your legs begins to transition from down to up, allow your legs to gently, slowly, and smoothly bounce during the space that your in-breath begins to change to out-breath. During this point of transition, from down to up, in to out, inhale to exhale, there's a sweet moment of weightlessness and timelessness as breath, energy, motion, and momentum converge; it manifests itself as a little bounce, similar to the one experienced in the last exercise.

As you complete the gentle bounce, begin breathing out as you sense the momentum in your legs pushing you up. As much as you can, "ride" on the momentum created by the downward motion. Convert the downward energy into upward energy by "bouncing" on the ball of energy that has been created by your breath, energy, and motion.

Breathe energy and awareness from the earth into your core as you begin to stand; just as your momentum carries you out of the gentle bounce to standing, visualize that you're consciously breathing

awareness-energy from the earth through the bottoms of your feet into the muscles of your ankles, knees, and thighs, actually propelling them into a standing position.

Use minimal muscle energy to lift your body upwards. Simultaneously, breathe energy-awareness from your core, through your heart center, and into your hands as your hands and arms begin to reverse their paths. Allow this energy-awareness to propel your arms and hands back along the same line that they traveled downward with as little consciously directed effort on your part as possible.

Breathe out slowly, smoothly, and continuously to a count of five. Activate your creative imagination and visualize your breath, awareness, energy, and motion being drawn right back along the same path that was initially "carved" by the original downward movement. In the same way that your lungs effortlessly reverse direction from inhaling to exhaling, sense that your body is able to reverse its direction, just as smoothly and seamlessly, from contraction to expansion.

As you breathe out through your mouth, allow the air to pass through your vocal chords without activating your voice as you did earlier, making that same voiceless "Ahhh…" sound. As you continue to breathe out in a slow, smooth stream of oxygen, sense that your hands are being drawn upwards by a force above your head. You can imagine this force as a pool or vortex of awareness, energy, intelligence, and compassion that has manifested just above you. This intelligent energy-awareness is drawing you, pulling your hands up as you continue to straighten your knees, keeping your back straight and aligned.

Follow your hands with your eyes. Notice how your hands seem to "scoop" energy from your heart center and carry it upwards toward the vortex that has manifested above your head and that lifts your hands and body upward with its magnetic pull. As your hands reach eye level, notice that they begin to naturally rotate from palms facing inwards to palms facing upwards. Allow this transition to occur naturally, effortlessly.

As your eyes continue to follow your hands upwards, again become aware of the muscle tension in the back of your neck when you begin to bend your head. Just notice the tension and allow your awareness to enter into the muscle itself.

Visualize, sense, and feel the release of frozen energy and cramped muscle tension as you allow your neck to relax, loosen, and soften with the upward motion of your head. Feel the hardened energy of chronic stress dissolve, liquefy, and circulate with the energy, breath, awareness, and motion that is Qi energy.

Imagine vital, flowing Qi energy being pulled up from the earth, into your core with your breath, through the center of your body, extending and circulating through your heart, into your arms, and out the palms of your hands, circulating and transforming frozen energy into flow energy.

As you completely discharge the last of your breath, allow your hands to fully extend up toward the sky with a slightly arched back and a small bend in your knees and elbows. Your eyes are pointed upwards, focused on your hands. The momentum of your upward physical energy is almost completely spent while your Qi energy continues to extend through your palms into the vortex of awareness, energy, intelligence, and compassion.

Empty yourself completely.

As you stand with hands and arms extended upward, your back slightly arched and in alignment with your center, your lungs empty and oxygen spent, allow your awareness to follow your breath and energy into the vortex. Imaginatively enter into this living, intelligent, aware, and compassionate field of energy.

For just the moment that you're suspended between out and in, expansion and contraction, allow the creative emptiness of your natural self to merge with this field of energy, awareness, and information.

Let go of the illusion of special-separateness and surrender to the joy of ordinary-oneness. Drink in fully from this life energy as you begin to take in another deep, energizing breath from your diaphragm. Continue with the natural flow of momentum as your breath, energy, and awareness begin again to collapse inward.

Allow yourself to surrender to this inward collapse. As you begin to open your diaphragm to fresh, revitalizing oxygen, drink in energy and awareness through your palms. Consciously pull your hands down toward your chest to a count of three, simultaneously allowing gravity to pull your center toward the earth.

Focus on the silver dollar spots in the middle of your palms that receive and transmit Qi energy. Allow your conscious awareness to surround and penetrate these energy centers as you pull your hands down from this vortex of pure energy and awareness. Can you feel a warmth or tingling there? Can you imagine these energy centers as small vortices of their own that actually do sense, absorb, and transmit energy?

As you pull your hands down, bend your knees and allow your center of gravity to sink with more force and momentum than the last movement. Allow the gravity of the earth to pull harder on your center by not resisting the pull as much with your legs. Allow the muscles in your legs to soften rather than resist. Keep your back straight and allow your core to sink with the movement of your center. Imagine your core as a ball of liquid-plasma energy about the size of a soccer ball right in the center of your body that "sloshes" with the movement of your center. This core energy actually is a kind of intelligence, even consciousness, that has "weight" and "presence," and that recognizes itself in, and as, the vortex of energy that's being pulled down and in by your palms.

As you simultaneously drop your center and pull down your hands to a count of three, focus your attention on the body-mind sensation-feeling of pulling energy from the vortex through your palms and down the center of your body into your core. As your hands flow down the centerline of your body, experience the sensation in your palms of actually pulling energy in and down with the "magnetic" movement of your hands. Imagine that your palms are pulling your internal Qi energy from the top of your head, down the center of your body, into your heart. Breathe this energy deeply into your heart and your core as you continue to inhale from your diaphragm.

When your hands reach chest level, allow your elbows and palms to flair out, so that there are about 24 inches between them, and pull your elbows back. Allow this movement to be carried on the momentum of your downward motion.

As your palms move away from each other, allow your attention to focus on the energy that you may be feeling in and between them. When your Qi begins to flow consciously through your body, you'll feel the silver dollar spots begin to heat up, vibrate, or itch. You may also have the sensation of a fluid, plasma energy flowing in and out of this spot with a very real physical sensation.

When your palms face each other, particularly when they're close together, you can feel the exchange of energy between them. As they begin to move apart, be sensitive to the sensation of this fluid, plasma-like energy stretching thinner and thinner the further apart you move them.

As your energy and momentum reach the bottom of the movement and come to a point of suspension, allow the fluid Qi energy to "slosh" or extend deep into your core and then begin to bounce back up much in the same way a yo-yo would begin to bounce up when thrown down. Sense the energy that has been stored in your legs from the brisk downward motion. As you reach the bottom of the motion, allow your awareness to enter into your legs and lower back. Can you sense the stored-up kinetic energy? Allow that static energy to convert into upward movement as you bounce your core energy into an upward thrust of your legs.

From your core, form an intention to extend your breath, awareness, energy, and motion through the center of your body and out the palms of your hands in a single, seamless motion. Mentally visualize and physically sense the smooth, flowing and coordinated movement of your body, lifting, standing, and extending as your breath is released to a count of four.

Consciously push your breath out from your diaphragm and control the flow of oxygen by constricting the muscles around your throat and vocal chords. As your air is being pushed out, simultaneously restrict the flow that's allowed through by tightening your throat and saying the word "Ahhh" without using your voice. You'll feel added tension in your diaphragm as this controlled stream of air escapes.

Allow your legs to release their stored-up kinetic energy as you begin to stand. Remember to keep your back straight so that your center is hovering and there's a straight line up from your core to your head.

As much as you can, surrender your individual force of ego-will to your body-mind. Allow the energy that's already active and present in your body to align itself with your core-intent to extend your energy and motion upwards. Give your body-mind, your Natural Self, permission to conduct and coordinate the movement.

As you consciously release your breath, allow your knees and legs to begin to straighten as if they had a mind of their own. Allow your body to follow your core intent to extend energy and awareness up through the palms of your hands into the vortex.

As your legs and knees begin to straighten in harmony with the releasing of your breath to a count of four, extend your awareness from your core to your hands as they begin again to come together, palms facing each other as the momentum of energy and motion reverse. In synchronization with your legs and breath, give over to the feeling or sensation that your hands have an awareness of their own. Besides being conductors of energy, the spots in the centers of your palms also sense energy.

Allow the awareness you feel in your core to extend and merge with the awareness you sense in your palms as your hands begin their upward motion. Springing on the momentum stored as kinetic energy in your legs, allow your arms and hands to ride on this cushion of energy as it extends upward.

As the energy of your core merges with the energy you feel in your palms, visualize that you're gently pushing energy from your core up the center of your body, into and through your heart, and finally up and out your palms into the vortex of energy.

Once again, empty yourself completely. As your palms reach upwards, your lungs empty, and your awareness extends into the energy vortex, allow yourself to experience the complete peace of silence, stillness, and emptiness in that timeless transition between out-breath and in-breath. In the silence of your being, sense your body's intent: does it want to draw in another Breath of Awareness?

Practicing Breath of Awareness

When you've practiced Breath of Relief for several days and can do it for three minutes continuously, having gotten over the initial soreness in your legs and back, you may be ready to begin Breath of Awareness. I hope you'll also consider trying Breath of Relief at work during those times you feel angry, frustrated, or tired. It's much better to let go of frozen energy before it sinks into body memory.

From your practice of Breath of Relief, you should begin to feel yourself more in your legs and lower body. One of the immediate benefits of FlowMotion™ is the feeling of energy and aliveness that will return to your body with practice. You might also begin to experience more body awareness.

Body awareness begins with feeling more connected to your body, more "inside" your body, more of the time. As you begin to practice Breath of Awareness, consciously become more open and receptive to the energies, feelings, sensations, even emotions and images that are always stored in and flowing through your body.

After you get comfortable doing the motions in harmony with your breathing, begin to allow your body awareness and intelligence to take over the job of directing each and every movement. Once you build a solid foundation (straight back, floating center, breathing from the diaphragm synchronously with your motion) you can begin to sense rather than think your way through each movement. As you begin to sense the flow of movement, allow your awareness to progressively focus inwards, to your inner experience. Without

thinking about it, allow your attention, the focus of your awareness, to turn from the outside of your body to the inside of your body as you do Breath of Awareness.

What does it feel like to be on the inside of your body as it flows in harmony with your breath from one movement to the next? Can you sense the movement as though you were the breath and energy that flows through your body? Can you sense your muscles as they push, pull, and float with each movement? Can you feel the aliveness in your nervous system as your back, spine, and neck gently stretch?

It may be helpful to focus on a particular part of your body or a specific muscle group as you practice Breath of Awareness. You might start with your legs and back, particularly if they're still sore. Rather than try to ignore the soreness or force movement in spite of the soreness, allow your awareness to surround the soreness and gently, easily breathe energy into that spot. Feed each part of your body with energy and awareness.

Each time you focus on a body part, become as open and receptive as you can to a different kind of language that your body speaks. This is the language of sensation, feeling, intuition, images, and hunches. Suspend the constant talk of the ego, look and listen to who you are, to the reality of your physical being.

Looking and listening, sensing and feeling, are the primary avenues of body awareness; notice, I didn't say talking or thinking. In fact, thinking (talking to ourselves) is the primary function of the ego, and it often prevents or blocks us from utilizing other sources of awareness. If you were to honestly and clearly compare the time you truly listen to yourself with the time you talk (think) to yourself, what do you think the percentage would be? Estimates are we spend 90 to 95 percent of the time talking and only 5 to 10 percent truly listening. How do you think you'd feel if you spent more time truly, empathically, non-judgmentally listening to yourself?

The more you're willing to suspend judgment and look and listen, the more you see and hear. You'll become aware of the subtle sensations, feelings, even emotions and images that you never realized were there. When you become truly receptive and open, you may find that your body actually does talk to you.

Practice Breath of Relief and Breath of Awareness together. After you've done three minutes of Breath of Relief (approximately 20 repetitions), allow your legs to rest. Breathe normally. When you feel strength returning to your legs do Breath of Awareness. Don't wait so long that you lose your sense of inner movement and momentum.

Continually listen to and follow the lead of your body's intelligence. Each time you practice these movements you learn to tune into the language of your body and your body releases and transforms stagnant and frozen energy into flow. Allow the intuition that's embedded in your body to guide your movements: look, listen, and learn.

Chapter Nine:

Breath of Acceptance

Genuine self-acceptance is actually a process of surrender and humility. This means surrendering to the actual, physical, here and now reality, not just the world you've created in your mind to soothe your narcissistic injuries and actualize a fantasy. Surrendering is giving in, not giving up.

Introduction: Acceptance, Surrender, and Humility: The Warrior's Way

The second gate of awareness in the Wu Ying Tao, the formless way system of Gung Fu that I'll explain more fully in the conclusion, is the Gate of Duality. This gate is guarded by the "Dragon of Fools," and to pass through this gate the Warrior must be humble, which probably explains why so few people actually make it through this gate.

The Gate of Duality is where much of the consciousness of our society lives today. This is the gate of ultimate good versus ultimate evil, completely right versus completely wrong, us versus them, this versus that. It's the binary language of computers where all information is ultimately reduced to zeros and ones.

In many ways we've reduced our living, spontaneous, and creative imagining, thinking, feeling processes into the lifeless routine of automatically categorizing all shades of color into black and white. After reducing the already limited amount of real knowledge that we have into lifeless categories, we have the tendency to then freeze and defend those categories with our most cherished need-desire, explained previously as the need to be right.

One of the greatest zones of blindness in my own perception is the tendency to place my ego in the center of the universe and actually expect that the universe should give me what I want, when I want it, and how I want it. My expectations of entitlement are often so automatic and in alignment with what our society tells me I should want, it's very difficult to identify them without a generous helping of self-honesty, or sometimes the rude awakening of getting repeatedly blindsided until I do wake up.

I had several experiences during my time in Singapore and Southeast Asia in which I discovered areas of blindness that I never even knew existed. Such discovery often requires that you consciously place yourself in a life situation that you've never been in before for you to really know where your areas of blindness are. The best sparring partner you can ever have are those unexpected, unprepared for life events if you're willing to open yourself up to new information and experiences a little bit outside your comfort zone.

Living in Singapore with my wife (a Chinese Singaporean) for several years forced me to look at many of the assumptions I took for granted, simply because I didn't know and I didn't know that I didn't know. There are many things Americans tend to take for granted until they actually spend some time living with, working with, and having friends who are local people in a culture very different than their own.

If you're willing to be honest with yourself, to transparently examine your feelings and perceptions and then take responsibility or ownership of them, your consciousness will necessarily undergo a transformation. This transformation can, and usually will, result in a radical shift of perception, from who you thought you were to a more honest, more realistic version of who you actually are.

One of the assumptions I took for granted was the idea of individual rights and freedoms. As an American, I just assumed it was the correct, inalienable right of every person to have the same kind of individual rights and freedoms that I enjoyed in the United States. What I learned was a real shock. My personal, misplaced expectations were being projected onto a people and culture I neither knew nor understood. Also, my very concept of "individualism" was cutting me off from my own energy. It's truly a shame that we've come to frame individualism as egotistic isolationism. The ego truly is a legend in its own mind, a very isolated, frightened, and lonely legend.

As explained more in-depth in previous chapters, the ego is locked in its protective, defensive isolation by the constant, pressing need to be right and the mortal fear and shame of being seen as wrong. People would rather face a firing squad than be shamed, which is why public speaking is the number one fear for most people.

The experience of shame is so painful for so many of us, the very thought of being publicly humiliated is mortifying. The experience of shame actually feels like being deeply wounded on an emotional level. When shame and blame are connected together and forcefully attributed to another person or event, the result can be self-fragmentation.

Self-fragmentation usually occurs between two opposite poles, grandiosity and devaluation. The more your sense of self fragments in response to intensely painful shame/blame attacks, the more you experience a duality form within your self-structure.

As a result of internalizing or "introjecting" raw, intensely painful and self-demeaning images, emotions, and sensations associated with the people, relationships, and experiences that precipitated the shame/blame reaction, a self-hating, self-blaming "island" of consciousness forms, comprised of images, sensations, and memories associated with the emotion or *Energy* in *MOTION* of shame and blame, another color of trauma and traumatic stress.

As a counter-measure to this powerful, painful, intrusive island of self-hate consciousness, the ego develops an equally unbalanced and unrealistic fantasy version of itself that's often revealed by its unquestioned expectations of entitlement. This fantasy self views itself as always right, always first, always best, and always deserving; it's the center of the universe and everyone else is simply expected to comply with its demands. It often resembles our mistaken concept of what it means to be "independent, important and special."

Genuine self-acceptance is actually a paradox. Many people consciously or unconsciously operate on the idea that they must stand out as an "individual" to be seen and noticed, must somehow possess or be something important, special, and different from the rest to be accepted by others, and therefore accepted by themselves. The more important and special you believe yourself to be, the greater your (fantasized) self-worth.

Genuine self-acceptance is actually a process of surrender and humility. This means surrendering to the actual, physical, here and now reality, not just the world you've created in your mind to soothe your narcissistic injuries and actualize a fantasy. Surrendering is giving in, not giving up.

True surrender is radical acceptance. It means giving into the reality that as an individual you're very small, even in terms of just this planet (not to mention the actual, true, real universe of immeasurable proportions existing for incomprehensible time). As one of billions of other people who share the same sun, water, oxygen, and energy, each of us stands out about as much as a single grain of sand on a huge beach.

Humility is the result of realizing and re-adjusting your sense of self-importance to more correctly fit your actual, true, real "size." A shocking realization for me as I was doing Qigong with my Sifu on the beach of Singapore was the sudden and forceful realization that the universe really doesn't revolve around my individual wants and needs. This planet and the others who exist here are not my personal playthings.

Humility is the Warrior's way. The only way to tame the Dragon of Fools is to be humble; it's the fool who pretends to be what he's not.

Humility also heals the split within the self. When you can be self-nurturing enough to be humble, you begin to accept and integrate all the parts of yourself that you've rejected and disowned. It's only when you can face up to who you really are without the ego-image of narcissistic self-importance that you can actually begin to change. Acceptance is the process of being good enough.

The Stance

To begin Breath of Acceptance, place your feet as you have in the last two exercises, a bit wider than shoulder width apart, knees bent, toes pointing forward as though you were riding an invisible horse. This time we're going to focus on developing physical and emotional balance, a dynamic and fluid balance. Dynamic or fluid balance is the result of the second-to-second process of accepting yourself, others, and life each on its own terms. To have dynamic balance is to be centered.

As you stand with your knees slightly bent, back straight, hands hanging loosely at your side, allow your attention to enter right into the center of your self. To help find your center, try closing your eyes, breathe deeply and slowly from your diaphragm and allow your attention to sink, all by itself. Resist the temptation to think your attention to where you believe it should be. Just allow it to seek its own level, to recognize and sense where it belongs and feels most centered.

Where does your attention go? Does it resist leaving the familiarity of your head, where the ego lives, continuing to identify with that separating entity? If you're having difficulty releasing your ego-head identification, focus your attention on your breath as it rises from your diaphragm as you inhale and sinks back into your diaphragm as you exhale. Focus on your breathing and let go of your thinking. What happens?

Can you feel your attention settling into a place within your body-mind self that feels natural? Can you glimpse the body-mind experience of your own natural self? Can you sense the very real and active intelligence of your natural body-mind self?

Glimpsing the Natural Self is an experience that's different than thinking about yourself as though you were an external object that can be evaluated and judged. It's more like sensing, feeling, and perceiving from within your natural body-mind continuum. In a way, it's a letting go of thinking, judging, and comparing as the only method to negotiate your sense experiences. Glimpsing requires the courage to be vulnerable enough to experience reality more directly.

As you allow your attention to center, what does it feel like? Can you feel a sense of emotional gravity where your attention is focused? Many people express a sense-feeling of internal presence when they allow their attention to settle within the core of their body-mind.

To help experience the weight of emotional gravity, give your physical center the experience of gravity by gently bouncing your body up and down a couple of times while focusing your attention on your core. Can you sense in your core this viscous, fluid-like plasma energy that extends down into your knees when you bounce down, and up into your heart center when you bounce up? This is the very real energy of Qi.

For the rest of the exercise, always keep one portion of your energy and attention focused in your core. Even though you will, at times, extend your attention and energy to other parts of your body-mind continuum, always allow one part of your attention to rest in the safety, security, and stability of your core. It's truly your home.

When you feel centered in your body and connected with the earth through the soles of your feet, make a slight bend at your elbows and extend your hands out to the left and right at shoulder height, palms facing out as though you were standing between two pillars, pushing on both of them.

Allow your attention to rest in your core and extend energy and attention to make a connection with both hands, first the left, then the right, then both simultaneously. Can you sense your energy and attention extending from your core out to both hands simultaneously? Close your eyes for a second to help visualize this flowing attention-energy extending from your core and connecting to your right and left hands. It's the focus of your intention that directs the energy of your attention.

Focus specifically now on the connection you feel between your right and left hands. Can you feel them with palms extended and facing outward? In what ways does your right hand feel similar to the left? Are they the same size, shape, weight, flexibility? Or, are there minor differences that you might be aware of? If both hands had separate personalities how would you describe them? Which hand is dominant? Would this be the more assertive leading personality? What about your non-dominant hand? Does it suffer from an inferiority complex? How much attention do you really give your non-dominant hand? How skillful is it in comparison to your dominant hand? What part of your personality would surface if you used only your non-dominant hand?

How does it feel to maintain a stance that holds both hands as far apart from each other as possible? Can you sense the duality you carry even in your physical body? Each part of your physical body, particularly each individual hand, represents some part of your psychological make-up as well. It's no wonder that children who have been physically or sexually abused tend to draw hands that are often too small, large, absent, misshapen, even grotesque.

Breath and Movement

Begin this breathing movement by first discharging the stagnant oxygen and energy that has accumulated over time from not fully discharging your *Energy* in *MOTION*.

To discharge the accumulated, stagnant oxygen-energy, sharply push inward on your lower stomach and diaphragm to fully exhale all of the stagnant air with a whoosh. Push it all the way out until you feel empty. As you push out the last of your stale oxygen, allow your awareness to connect your core breathing with your arms and hands. What do you notice? Can you sense your arms and hands wanting to move with the action of exhaling? Try it again.

When you vigorously push the remaining oxygen from your lungs with arms extended, can you sense the energy that automatically travels with your breath from your core to your hands? Do your arms and hands naturally want to push out? Allow and exaggerate the movement. Allow your arms and hands to be moved simply by the energy that is your breath.

After you discharge this stagnant oxygen-energy, allow your diaphragm to open and slowly drink in the new, fresh, and vital oxygen-energy that flows outside your body. Allow the vacuum created by pushing out the breath to draw in new oxygen to the slow count of four. Relax into the breath so that you don't feel rushed or desperate to quickly fill yourself. Learn to tolerate and eventually master the feeling of mild discomfort associated with not immediately having what you feel you need.

Continue to be centered in your core with energy and attention extended to your right and left hands as you slowly draw in a breath. In synchronous harmony with your breath, allow the core energy of your attention, your intention, to draw both hands inward toward your heart. As your hands are drawn in, allow your arms to relax as much as you can so that the sensation of volitional movement arises from your core rather than your mind.

What do you notice about the movement of your hands? Are they moving together in unison? Does one hand want to go faster than the other? How balanced and coordinated do they feel? Is there more attention-energy in one hand over the other? How connected does either hand feel with your core and breath?

In harmony with the movement of your hands and breathing, consciously squeeze the muscles of your legs as you lower your center of gravity. Remember to keep your back straight by arching it just slightly so that the top half of your body doesn't bend forward as you lower your center. Stay as suspended in your center as possible.

As you remain connected between your core and hands, extend some of your energy and awareness to the large muscles in your legs. As you lower your center of gravity, flex the large muscles in your legs. This will draw a springing energy into those muscles. Continue to allow your core-intent to draw your right and left

hands closer and closer to each other in a scooping motion as you fill your lungs with oxygen and energy. What is your experience of drawing together two separate yet (distantly at times) connected parts of your body-mind together? Can you feel the accumulation of energy in your arms and hands from the motion of scooping?

As your lungs become full of oxygen and your center is drawn as close as it can comfortably go toward the earth, allow your right and left hands to continue to swing so that they cross in front of your heart center. As the momentum in your hands continues to carry the motion forward, allow your right and left hand to continue to cross in front of your heart center and begin an upward motion, palms facing outwards as your lungs become full of oxygen. Pause for a moment of suspended energy and attention in that sweet place where right is left and left is right.

When the momentum of the energy stored in your arms and hands reaches the turning point, allow that energy to transform into an expressive energy as you begin to release your breath. Release your breath to a count of four, simultaneously releasing the energy stored in your arms and legs.

As the momentum in your legs begins to change from down to up, allow your legs to gently, slowly, and smoothly bounce during the space that your in-breath is transitioning to out-breath. Take a second to recognize and enjoy this sweet spot in between change.

Exhale your breath with controlled force as you activate the muscles of your arms and legs to spring back to the starting position. Breathe out in a controlled, intense stream of oxygen to a count of four as you straighten your arms and legs. As you begin to straighten your knees, consciously tighten your quadriceps and slowly push the center of your body up with your legs. Tightening the leg muscles in harmony with releasing breath will stimulate and activate your body awareness.

In conjunction with the previous movements, breathe energy into your arms as you allow the energy in your hands to be released and transformed into outward, expressive movement. As you begin to stand up, breathe oxygen and energy in and through your hands as they reverse direction and begin to travel away from each other.

Feed your expressive, outwardly directed energy and motion with your breath and from your core. Continue to keep some part of

your attention-energy focused in your core. Even as you feed your motions with breath and energy, imagine that you're extending your core energy and awareness into your body by consciously "feeding" and nourishing your sense of self with breath and energy. Allow your awareness to imaginatively enter into the "mind" of your hands as they begin to flow out to the left and right. What was each hand's experience of collecting, intertwining, and now expressing Energy in MOTION? Do your hands feel any different in the outward expressive motion than they did during the energy-collecting inward motion? Are your hands in any way changed from their exchange of energy?

Continue to consciously breathe awareness, energy and motion from your core through your legs, arms, and hands as you push your energy and awareness through the energy vortices in the middle of your palms. As your hands reach the point in their outward movement where your palms are again facing out to the left and right as though you were about to push on pillars to either side of you, tighten the muscles in your arms and forcefully exhale the remainder of your breath through your throat with a silent "Hahhhh."

As the last of your breath rushes out, finish the upward thrust from your legs as your hands and arms become fully extended. Remember to always keep elbows and knees slightly bent, even at the end, or beginning, of each exercise. One of the reasons so many people have elbow and knee problems is because of the residual energy that is stored there from over-extension.

As you extend your palms, release the tension completely from your arms and legs and allow the Qi energy to rush out the silver dollar spots in your palms. As you suddenly and consciously relax your physical tension, you release the Qi energy that was stored in your body and breath.

Extend your Qi energy through your palms, out away from your body, and into the external environment by consciously sensing and imagining an almost sticky, plasma-like energy extending through the silver dollar spots in the middle of your palms. Imagine and sense in your hands this electric/elastic energy shooting out your palms in concert with the final thrust of your breath and motion.

Continue to imaginatively follow this energy. What happens to it as the oxygen in your lungs empties out, the momentum in your movements becomes completely extended, and you can begin to sense the transition of outward movement into an inward movement of breath, energy, and motion? Can you intuitively sense the rebound of energy as your hands begin the inward journey?

Assist your intuition and imaginatively visualize that the energy that was extended out is being pulled back in with even more energy as you begin a deep, powerful breath from your diaphragm to a short count of four.

Imagine that the initial outward thrust of energy doesn't actually dispel and weaken, but transforms and attracts energy with a similar positive charge, returning back through your palms as your diaphragm creates the vacuum to draw in more breath and energy.

Join with this returning energy as you consciously open your lower lungs by extending your abdomen to assist a full and expedient intake of oxygen and energy. As you begin to pull oxygen into your lungs, open your heart center to absorb and metabolize the invigorating and nourishing energy-information.

As you pull in your hands and arms with a scooping motion, visualize that you're "scooping" energy with your hands into your heart center in harmony with your in-breath. You can visualize this energy exchange as a pouring of light plasma from each palm into the heart center as they begin to cross so that right becomes left and left becomes right.

Allow your awareness to extend from your core into your heart-center as energy from your palms is being exchanged and transmuted. Can you sense this energy vortex in the middle of your chest? Do you sense the connection between your heart-center and *Energy in MOTION?* Can you feel an absorption and transmutation of energy as your right palm crosses the left side of your heart-center and your left palm crosses the right?

While you vigorously absorb your in-breath, lower your center of gravity by consciously squeezing your quadriceps and bending your knees, keeping your lower back slightly arched. Visualize and feel your body to be a strong and resilient spring as you coil inward, absorbing in-flowing energy.

When your lungs are full and your hands have reached the apex of their swing, allow your complete attention to focus on the moment

inhale changes to exhale and outward flowing energy and motion changes to inward flowing. Immerse yourself completely in the experience of feeling full, enough, whole, and complete. This is a "glimpsing" of your Natural Self. Absorb and internalize this moment into your core.

As the momentum of your inward motions, the fullness of your breath and energy, transitions to an outward flow, slowly and consciously release your body tension with your breath to a slow count of four.

As your hands begin their down-outward movement, uncrossing in front of your heart-center, allow your palms to again be sensitive to absorbing and circulating your heart-energy. Sense, imagine, and visualize that you can drink in this living, intelligent, and nourishing heart energy through the silver dollar spots in the middle of your palms as your hands slowly, lightly, and effortlessly float on this energy.

Allow your hands and arms to uncross in front of your heart center and begin to flow out to the left and right, while simultaneously inviting your center to rise by extending energy and awareness from your core to your legs and back.

As you place your attention in your knees, legs, and back, breathe energy into the muscles, effortlessly activating them to contract into a standing motion. As much as you're able, allow your legs to stand by themselves without your "making it happen." Allow and invite the motion to happen on its own as you breathe energy into your legs.

While your center flows up with the slow, smooth, exhaling of your breath, allow your arms and hands to move in harmony. As your hands reach the point where both palms are facing out to the left and right, completely surrender to the out-flowing *Energy in MOTION.*

For the remainder of the movement, allow your mind to go completely quiet as your energy, attention, and intention seamlessly focus in becoming the out-flowing energy that extends through your palms to the left and right. Extend your breath, energy, and awareness in opposite directions while remaining centered and connected to your core. Experience the sensation of being separate and connected at the same time.

In this place of stillness and quiet, allow yourself to glimpse the unity behind duality. By surrendering the need to be right, better, or more special than others, you can halt your ego's continuous, compulsive comparison and judgment that's at the root of binary thinking and come to a different understanding and perception. You can seed the field of potential for a radical acceptance and transformation.

Practicing Breath of Acceptance

Practice Breath of Acceptance in the same way you practice Breath of Relief and Breath of Awareness.

By now you should be developing some strength and resilience in your legs and back. When you're able to do three minutes of Breath of Relief, followed by a short rest and then three minutes of Breath of Awareness, your back and legs should have built up some strength. In the same way as you added Breath of Awareness to Breath of Relief, add Breath of Acceptance to your routine until you're able to do each movement for three minutes with a short rest in between.

When practicing Breath of Acceptance, allow your awareness to begin the exercise from a perception-position of duality, separateness. As you have your hands extended to the left and right, extend awareness energy from your core to each hand separately. Experience them as right then left or even right versus left. Allow your awareness to sense and absorb the differences in awareness with each hand.

Each hand represents the two polarities of yourself: right and left, dominant and non-dominant, north and south, male and female, idealized and devalued, Yin and Yang. Each hand has its own center of awareness and perception, its own separate past history of interaction with the world, and each has learned different lessons from these interactions.

In martial arts it becomes immediately clear that you favor one part of your body over another; the dominant hand tends to be much stronger, faster, and more coordinated than the non-dominant. The dominant hand has received the majority of your attention and energy and as a result you have a better relationship with that hand. It responds faster and better to your conscious intention than your non-dominant hand.

The non-dominant hand has been starved for attention and energy and as a result, it's weaker, slower, and doesn't respond as immediately to conscious intent. In some ways you could say the dominant hand is idealized while the non-dominant is devalued.

Train your attention to notice these differences in the way that you extend your hands, the way in which you sense the energy and awareness, or a lack thereof, in your hands, how strong, connected, and coordinated they feel.

When you pull your hands in toward your center, allow your attention to focus on each hand separately and then together. Extend energy and awareness from your core into both hands simultaneously. What do you notice? Can you begin to sense a convergence of right hand energy-awareness with left hand energy-awareness?

Even as your palms approach each other notice how heat, pressure, and energy flow out from the vortex in each hand, intermix, and flow into the vortex of the opposite hand. As your hands cross each other in the movement, can you sense the energy-awareness exchange?

Can you imagine all of the experiences that have been stored in the right side of your brain and body flowing out of your right palm and into your left, while all of the experiences that have been stored in the left side of your brain and body flow into your right palm?

Breath of Acceptance is your body-mind's natural way to integrate and synthesize the opposing, conflicting, dualistic nature of thinking and perceiving that's so accepted in our society that it silently takes root in your body, even your muscle memory. Acceptance is awareness. Acceptance is also essential for transformation.

Each time you practice Breath of Acceptance, allow your awareness to progressively take ownership of your body-mind. Connect motions, movements, breath, momentum, core, heart, and head in a symphony of energy and flow. Integrate and heal the split between idealized and devalued, left and right, us and them. Open your heart to the possibility of glimpsing a different reality.

Chapter Ten:

Breath of Transformation

The magic of transformation is often the unexpected, unprepared for way in which it occurs. The process of transformation is the ability to let go of what you think you know in order to glimpse a different reality.

Introduction: The Magic of Transformation

Personal transformation really is magical; I've experienced it in various forms personally and have witnessed it in multiple forms as a mental health therapist. The magic of transformation is often the unexpected, unprepared for way in which it occurs. The process of transformation is the ability to let go of what you think you know in order to glimpse a different reality.

Glimpsing is the experience of catching, out of the corner of your eye, an entirely different perspective from anything you could personally imagine. The moment you try to look directly at the experience, to try to rationally understand what's happening, to impose some sort of form on it, you lose the experience.

One of my personal experiences of transformation occurred as I was practicing Qigong with my Sifu in Singapore at a place called East Coast Parkway, famous for Chili Crab. It was early morning as the sun was rising on the horizon of the South China Sea. I had just finished the physical movements of Qigong and was holding an energy stance when a sudden and radical transformation occurred in how I perceived myself in relation to my reality.

For several months leading up to this experience, I practiced Qigong with Sifu almost every morning in the park or sometimes in the afternoon at one of the police headquarters with some of the men in his charge as an inspector with the Singapore Police Department. The practice of Qigong is very subtle yet very powerful, and over a couple of months it began to precipitate some changes in my body, emotions, and perceptions.

Like many people in the helping professions, I've experienced traumatic stress in childhood and secondary traumatic stress working with trauma survivors. Also, like many care providers, I struggled with severe and persistent depression. Despite being very active physically, and a long time meditator, my depression did at times overwhelm me, even resulting once in a serious suicide attempt.

Years of therapy and Prozac later I felt more stable yet quite reliant upon Prozac to keep my depression at bay, until I began the conscious breathing and mindful movement of Qigong. Doing Qigong on a regular basis, particularly when I was able to practice next to the ocean or some other large energy source, began to "loosen" the frozen, restricted energy that was locked into my body. At times I would feel tears rushing down my face, or my legs would shake and my abdomen and pelvis would tremble when holding the energy stance.

Over the weeks and months of practice, I would sometimes experience rapidly shifting states of consciousness, vivid dreams, changes in appetite and energy levels. My wife told me she heard me singing in my sleep one night "I love Qigong, I love Qigong." Even these experiences didn't prepare me for what was about to happen, though.

This particularly beautiful morning we had just finished the series of six exercises and I had taken a rather precise stance where your feet are right at shoulder width, knees and feet bent slightly inwards. Your back is held straight, arms and hands held out similar to the starting position for Breath of Relief, except wider with fingers spread apart.

When you're able to hold this stance for some period of time, focusing on your breath, a kind of involuntary shaking will begin to happen in your legs. It usually starts with the knees and travels into the legs and sometimes even into the pelvis and core. If you just allow the movement to happen without judging, tensing, or trying to control it, you will experience a type of energy discharge that's very difficult to describe.

It's simultaneously a releasing, a transformation, and a re-integration of frozen-in-fear *Energy* in *MOTION*, memory fragments, and body sensations. It's as though each fragment of the traumatic experience that had been held, frozen in time, was released from its isolated bondage into the light to transform and re-integrate as part of a whole, living, flowing core energy.

This time the shaking and trembling didn't stop in my legs, abdomen, or core. It seemed to travel right up the center of my body, through my heart, and out the top of my head. Right at that point my perception flipped inside out.

Rather than perceiving myself as large and in the center of the universe, I shrunk and became very, very, very, small, absolutely tiny, the size of a grain of sand on a huge beach. It was very clear at that moment that I'm not the center of the universe. I'm not nearly so large, important and special as my ego-perception would have me believe. I am in fact quite small and ordinary in the context of our actual, true, physical reality.

I can't tell you the sense of relief that came with this revelation. I was suddenly set free! For those few precious moments, and to some degree the rest of that day, and to a slighter degree even now, I was freed from the bondage of my self-importance, from the need to be right.

At that moment, I realized in my bones that much of my personal suffering was self-imposed by my need to be special, whether it was specially good or specially bad really didn't matter. I was convinced that my very life depended upon being seen, noticed, and needed as special, different, apart, better than the rest. I left no room in my self-image to be ordinary, or just "good enough." At that moment I released my depression and dependence upon Prozac.

Glimpsing a different reality, even for just a moment, can be life changing. Even though the solidity of that reality can fade over time as you slip back into ordinary consciousness, the memory remains. Most importantly, it lets you know, without a doubt in your mind, that there are other ways in which to perceive yourself, others, and even the fabric of life itself.

The Stance

In this state, gravity is experienced not as a force pulling you down, but as an energy filling you up. There is no need to fight gravity, for it fills you with energy. Thus, a very basic conflict, that of trying to escape the pull of gravity, is dissolved and turned inside out. Ending this conflict has vast emotional, psychological and health benefits.

— Bob Klein, *Movements of Magic,* page 8

To find your center in Breath of Transformation, place your conscious awareness in your feet as you stand with them in the Horse Stance, the same position as you begin each exercise. Allow your awareness to firmly connect with your feet on the ground, particularly your soles. Can you imagine the "souls of your feet?"

What do you notice as you place your attention in the soles of your feet? Can you feel your presence in your soles? In which part? Can you sense a spot, about the size of a silver dollar on the bottom center of your feet, similar to the vortices in your palms? Visualize with your body-sense, a warm, tingling, mild pressure on the center-bottom of both feet. Can you sense, feel, or visualize it? This is the energy exchange between your feet, gravity, and the earth. In *Movements of Magic,* Bob Klein explains that "Rather than a pulling down, your experience [in the stance described above] is one of a dynamic connectedness. Earth energy is shooting up through your legs and roots are growing down into the Earth, drinking up every drop of energy they can find."[1]

Visualize with your eyes closed that you can sense energy roots, from the bottom of both feet, extending down into the earth. You can imagine these roots as the same kind of plasma energy that comprises your core. Visualize and sense in your soles an energy that connects you with the earth, feeding your internal core. In a very real way, each person is an extension of the earth's core energy.

As you take in a deep, energetic breath from your diaphragm, picture that you're pulling vital energy through those visualized roots. As you inhale to a count of four, sense in your soles a continual flow of energy from the earth that extends up through the silver dollar spots on the bottom of your feet, through your ankles, knees, and legs, and into your core. Allow the energy to continue extending from your core, connecting to your heart center, up through your throat, and finally out the top of your head to a vortex of living, intelligent, awareness-energy. Can you imaginatively enter into this stream of flowing, nourishing, renewing energy? How does it make you feel to visualize this energy flowing from the earth through your core and out of your mind?

When your inhalation naturally transforms to exhalation, allow your lungs to slowly release your breath and reverse the flow of

---

[1] Bob Klein, *Movements of Magic,* page 8

energy to a count of six. Allow your breath to slowly and smoothly escape in a controlled stream of oxygen from your mouth. Visualize the flow of energy extending and connecting from the vortex, through the top of your head, and to your heart center, then from your heart center, to your core, through your legs and knees, and out the bottoms of your feet, deep into the earth.

Breathe several breaths consciously in this way, allowing the energy to flow up and down the middle of your body-mind. Can you begin to sense the body feeling associated with the circulation of energy? Allow your body to begin to mimic the flow of the energy that you feel. What does your body want to do? Can you sense a rhythm in your knees that wants to gently extend up with your in-breath and bend down on the out-breath? Allow your body to do this for a couple of breaths. Let yourself get into the flow and rhythm. As you get into this kind of rhythm, pay attention to your hands and arms. What do they want to do? Give your arms and hands permission to do whatever they want to do within the gentle rhythm of your breathing-motion. What do they do?

How difficult is it for you to let go and let your body move on its own? The more you're able to surrender your need for personal control over your breath, energy, and motion, the more you'll be able to flow effortlessly. Learn to trust your intuition by listening to the subtle music of energy and information that constantly plays through your Natural Self.

Breath and Movement

Momentum is felt as slow-motion waves flowing through the body. As an arm moves to the right, a wave of momentum slowly spreads through it until, reaching the fingertips, the wave slowly bounces back through the center of the body and perhaps into the opposite leg, which steps out next. Thus, these waves of momentum splash in slow motion from one part of the body through the center and into another part.

— Bob Klein, *Movements of Magic*, pages 6-7

Continue in the Horse Stance with both hands extended six inches out in front of your chest, palms facing each other with fingers held loosely. Allow your wrists and elbows to relax and hang loosely.

As you begin to fully discharge the stagnant oxygen that can accumulate in your lungs from years of shallow, incomplete breathing, allow your center of gravity to sink in harmony with your stream of breath. As your center sinks down, allow your arms and hands to sink with the same motion as if they were being pulled by the gravity of the earth. As you slowly and smoothly discharge your breath, allow your hands to flow down the centerline of your body, palms six inches apart and facing each other. What do you notice as your palms do this in concert with the outflow of your breath and the lowering of your center of gravity? Can you sense-feel the energy in your palms connecting with the energy running through the center of your body-mind? Can you feel the pull in your palms as you draw your hands down the middle of your heart-center?

Engage your creative imagination to visualize with your felt-sense that your hands, particularly your palms, are actually pulling energy through the center midline of your body with this slow, fluid, downward motion. See and feel the downward circulation of core energy through the center of your body.

As you continue to slowly discharge all of your oxygen by pushing out from your diaphragm, allow your hands to sink down past your abdomen, palms rotating toward the ground, until you have just a slight bend in your elbows. Fully participate in this letting-go motion by releasing a silent "Ahhh…" with your breath as you empty yourself of all of your un-discharged, residual breath-energy. At the same time, allow your center to sink with the bending of your knees until your energy and momentum are fully, easily, and naturally extended into the earth. Your knees are bent, your back is straight, your hands are extended with a slight bend in your elbows, and your palms are facing toward the earth. All of the downward momentum has been discharged with your breath through the energy portals in the soles of your feet and the palms of your hands.

Allow yourself to experience an extension of your conscious awareness. As you feel the momentum of your movement continue its downward-inward path, even after the physical motion has stopped, allow your awareness to extend through your palms and soles into the earth with your momentum.

Sense, feel, and visualize this momentum-energy extending into the ground. Can you imagine energy extending through the palms of your hands and the soles of your feet into the earth? Can you sense the earth's energy? What happens as you extend your personal, individual energy into the collective, universal energy of the earth?

As your energy extends with your breath and motion, it will also lose its downward momentum just a brief moment after your breath and motion have stopped. It's precisely this point that the energy-momentum extends into the earth as though it were elastic; just as this ball of elastic plasma energy reaches the end of its forward momentum, it begins to spring back as if it were a yo-yo that was thrown in a downward motion.

As your breath transitions from exhaling to inhaling, pause in that sweet zone of weightless, timeless, emptiness where time and motion stand still and silent. It's in this zone of transition that you'll often have your best opportunity to glimpse a different reality. As your diaphragm easily and naturally begins expanding to fill the void with fresh oxygen and energy, sense the rebound of your energy back up from the earth and into the soles of your feet and the palms of your hands.

Consciously breathe in the energy. Breathe through the energy vortices in the center of your soles and palms as you draw, in and up, the immense energy of the earth. As you slowly and smoothly begin to straighten your knees in harmony with a slow, deep, even breath to a count of four, visualize that you're drinking in the earth's vital energy through your hands and feet. Consciously and deliberately, draw this living, intelligent energy up into your core.

Allow your hands to begin their upward motion in harmony with your in-breath. As you breathe in to a slow count of four, begin to pull your hands apart and up with the fingers of the right and left hand pointing toward each other. Imagine that you're drawing your arms up and out as if you were to begin a graceful swan dance. Hold your wrists, hands, and elbows loosely.

As your hands follow the upward arc set by your elbows, you can easily imagine that you're a maestro conducting the music of your Natural Self, pulling deep chords of energy from the earth, through your legs, and into your core. You can also sense the connection of energy between your core and your hands, as your palms pull this plasma energy into the shape of an upward arc.

Begin to straighten your knees, keeping your back straight and aligned. As your hands continue their upward arc, imagine this pulling motion drawing energy upwards from your core, through the center of your body, yet remaining connected to the energy vortices in your palms. This drawing motion also feels as though

you're pulling your weight or gravity up through your center so that you actually feel lighter. Your knees straighten automatically and harmoniously with the movement.

As your elbows reach chest level and you're about halfway through your in-breath, allow your hands to naturally rotate with the movement of your arms as they begin to reach, rather than pull, upwards. Allow your hands to begin to reach in an upward arcing motion as your palms simultaneously begin to face each other, fingers held loosely and slightly apart from each other.

Continue to glide on the momentum of your upward, drawing motion. As you pull energy up from your core, through the middle of your body, and into your heart center, feel it collect in your hands. It will feel as though your hands actually have more gravity, as if they were magnetized and you were pulling iron filings with your magnetic field.

As your hands begin to reach in harmony over your head, allow them to be pulled toward each other, palm to palm, as if they were magnetically drawn. Simultaneously, experience the upward flow of energy from your heart-center to the crown of your head, as your lungs become full and nourished with fresh, vital, oxygen and energy.

At the point your hands are suspended over your head, palm to palm about six inches apart, your legs are fully extended with a slight bend in your knees, your back is slightly arched, and your lungs are full of oxygen, allow your in-breath to seamlessly transition to out-breath. Suspend your attention and allow your awareness to hover at this transition point from fullness back toward emptiness.

Allow the breath to flow out from your throat, through your mouth, in a voiceless "Ahhh…" sound to a count of five. Control the volume and intensity of your oxygen by squeezing those inner throat muscles that restrict the passage of air through your larynx. To a count of six, pull your palms from above your head down the centerline of your head and body with the same intensity that you use to let out your breath.

With the absence of physical tension or force, begin to intensely pull your palms straight down the center of your forehead. What's your experience? Can you feel the same intensity in your hands and arms that you experience when you push the oxygen from your diaphragm through the restricted opening in your throat? What's your experience of intensity absent the tension?

Continue to pull your hands down the centerline of your head and face as you lower your center of gravity by bending your knees. As you bend your knees, visualize that you're "collapsing in" toward your center. Allow the downward pull of your hands, energy, and the earth to pull your center of gravity down and in, while continuing to keep your back straight and aligned.

Can you feel the connection between the earth, your core, your hands, and the energy that's magnetically drawn down through you with the motion of your palms?

Begin to follow your hands with your eyes when they're at eye level. As your hands begin to descend past your face to heart level, feel the stretching in the back of your neck as you follow your hands with your eyes. Consciously allow the muscles in the back of your neck and shoulders to stretch and relax.

Continue to bend your knees to whatever level is comfortable and appropriate for you. By the time your hands have reached your abdomen, your knees should be fully bent and your center as low to the ground as it can comfortably be. Your hand-arm movement will also be at a point of transition, from pulling to pushing. As your hands become parallel with your elbows, extended just out from your abdomen, your pulling down motion will smoothly and seamlessly transition into a pushing down motion. Continue the motion past your abdomen and into your core center.

You'll experience a compression of energy in your core from the downward momentum of your Qi running into your fully bent knees and lowered center of gravity that act as an "energy-coil." The compression of this energy-coil feels like pushing on a soft, springy, resilient ball of plasma energy that playfully springs back when compressed. As you experience this compression of Qi energy begin to coil in your core, discharge the last of your oxygen with a drawn out "Ahhh" until your lungs are completely empty. Allow some dynamic tension in your abdomen as you consciously squeeze out the last of your oxygen.

At the moment of transition of breath and momentum, allow a second attention to emerge from the core of your being. As your ego-awareness is mystified by the glimpse of a different reality, allow your attention to sink into the core of your body-mind, your Natural Self. Imaginatively enter into the place in your body where you intuitively feel centered and connected, into the vortex and connection of your energy-awareness.

In this moment of time-energy-motion suspension, surrender your individual, in-your-head, "center of the universe" perception of yourself. Suspend the ego's voice and listen with your heart and gut.

Can you sense another awareness, a second attention that emanates from a point at the core-center of your body? It's a core-awareness, an in-your-bones intelligence that gently whispers to you and sometimes nudges you with its intuition and hunches. It's an intelligence that often speaks with body sensations, intuitive feelings, images, and direct perception rather than sequential, "rational" thought.

To the extent that you're able, glimpse this different reality. Be consciously receptive to a more direct perception of your whole body-mind self. Let go of the need to analyze and allow your self a more honest and clear perception of your here and now, in your body experience.

Practicing Breath of Transformation

Practice Breath of Transformation after you're able to do two minutes of each of the other breaths with only a short rest in between. By now your legs and back should be fairly strong and getting prepared for the next step of being able to do the entire FlowMotion™ exercise.

To practice the Breath of Transformation (as well as the whole of FlowMotion™) is to invoke transformation through consciously circulating energy and awareness throughout the body. The very act of conscious breathing and mindful movement are in themselves transformational. I don't believe it's possible not to evolve into a more conscious, creative, joyful being when practicing FlowMotion™; the motions themselves are the expression, the spontaneous, creative play of the Natural Self.

Breath of Transformation is the final movement in FlowMotion™ and is the synthesis and integration of the energy, awareness, and motion that has been generated by the last three movements. When practiced as a whole, unbroken, flowing motion, each breathing movement activates, circulates, and evolves Qi energy through certain "Gates of Transformation:" Blindness, Duality, Oneness, and Emptiness.

Each "Gate" is a point of energy-awareness perception. As your Qi energy "evolves" through the practice of FlowMotion™, your energy and perception will also begin to expand and transform. Each transformation begins as a glimpse into a different way of perceiving yourself in relation to your reality.

Breath of Transformation is a portal, a point of entrance into a different perception of yourself in relation to your internal and external realities. Each time you pull your hands, arms and elbows up, be as sensitive as you can to your internal core Qi energy that circulates up in conjunction with your limbs through the center of your body.

Can you visualize the motion of your pulling palms drawing energy from your core, into your heart center, into your head, and finally out the top of your head as your hands reach in harmony above you? Can you also visualize your palms pulling this energy from your abdomen in an upward arc? Do you sense any changes in the quality of energy or your perception as you perform this motion?

Energy and perception are simply two sides of the same quantum coin. As your energy transforms you'll begin to look at yourself, your life, and others in subtly different ways. Over a period of time practicing Breath of Transformation and FlowMotion™, your perception will evolve, from experiencing yourself as alone and special, as the middle of your personal universe, to perceiving yourself as a small, ordinary, yet deeply connected and vital part of the shared universe.

Chapter Eleven:

The Magic of FlowMotion™

Flow is a state of self-forgetfulness, the opposite of rumination and worry: instead of being lost in nervous preoccupation, people in flow are so absorbed in the task at hand that they lose all self-consciousness, dropping small preoccupations — health, bills, even doing well — of daily life. In this sense moments of flow are egoless.

— Daniel Goleman, *Emotional Intelligence*, page 91

Introduction: The Science of Flow

I wrote pretty extensively about flow in previous chapters, but I'd like to return to the subject again, briefly, before I explain the interconnectedness of each part of FlowMotion™, the final movements that will bring you back and help you center yourself after the activity and movement.

I use the word "flow" very specifically. To reiterate, it's a state of being fully engaged, mentally, physically, emotionally aware of the in the body, here and now experience of existence. Many people have different descriptions of this state, from athletes to those engaged in religious mysticism to artists who find themselves in the midst of some sort of state of total internal focus.

Flow really is on the opposite end of the mind-body continuum from Compassion Fatigue. Whereas Compassion Fatigue is characterized by being lost in rumination and worry, flow opens your mind and connects you back to your body. Whereas Compassion Fatigue can result in decreasing concentration and focus, flow aligns and focuses intention with attention. Can you imagine doing something excellently, simply for the enjoyment of doing it?

Flow is known to athletes as peak performance, "the zone." It's a highly energized and enjoyable state of physical and mental harmony, characterized by confidence, control, and awareness. As stated before, flow isn't just for athletes. It's for anyone who becomes lost in the moment of an activity that's done solely for the sake of process, rather than progress. It's when the self and the psyche totally integrate.

In my seminars on transforming Compassion Fatigue into flow I ask participants how and when they experience flow in everyday life. People often reply that playing a musical instrument, writing, engaging in a hobby, sport, or other challenging physical or mental activity engages them in a sense of flow.

Almost everyone is able to describe times in which they experience this state. What they're often unable to describe is how they entered it and how to get back into it consciously and purposefully. It appears we enter into flow states spontaneously and often don't bring the recognition of that flow back with us into our usual state of Compassion Fatigue.

Interestingly, almost no one associates flow with work until those conditions that can result in flow are specifically identified. Then the flow that has always been available at work is recognized. We most likely experience more flow at work than we selectively remember when we get home.

One suggestion I'd like to pass along right now is the next time you experience that sense of flow, whether it's at work, home, or on vacation, *drink that experience in to your core!* We're so unconsciously attuned to negative energy that we eat it like candy. Begin to become conscious of those moments when you experience that deep, in-your-bones absorption and enjoyment. Without disturbing the experience, allow yourself to absorb and internalize, even metabolize, the richness of the moment. Allow these precious moments to begin to form the basis of your Natural Self-perception.

As you become more physically, mentally, and emotionally sensitized to the experience of flow, you may find that flow has these operating principals working along with it.

1. Focus. One of the first operating principles of flow is the ability to establish and maintain focus. In fact, flow may very well be the result of your ability to maintain focused attention. In *Emotional Intelligence,* Daniel Goleman explains that "Flow is a state devoid of emotional static, save for a compelling, highly motivating feeling of mild ecstasy. That ecstasy seems to be a by-product of the attentional focus that is a prerequisite of flow. Indeed, the classic literature of contemplative traditions describe states of absorption that are experienced as pure bliss: flow induced by nothing more than intense concentration."[1]

2. Concentration on the Task at Hand. Closely related to focus is concentration. Real and pure concentration is related to the state of fascination. We concentrate best when we're deeply interested, involved, and relaxed, a state of focused absorption.

---

[1] Daniel Goleman, *Emotional Intelligence,* page 92

Dr. Goleman: "A strained concentration — a focus fueled by worry — produces increased cortical activation. But the zone of flow and optimal performance seems to be an oasis for cortical efficiency, with a bare minimum of mental energy expended."[2]

3. Absorption. Absorption is a state of continual, focused concentration that manifests when challenges and skills are in balance. Your whole skill set must be used to meet a particular task, a task that's perfect for you because it demands every single skill that you have in your set, nothing more, nothing less. Because your talents have been balanced with the activity at hand, absorption becomes natural.

4. The Merging of Action and Awareness. Another principle associated with flow is the merging of who you are with what you're doing. This requires a complete surrender to the immediate experience of the activity at hand. In deep states of flow there's sometimes a blurring between the subjective and objective experience. Rather than doing the activity, the activity at times seems to be doing you.

5. The Paradox of Control. It's a paradox: the more you need control, the less control you experience yourself to have. The more you're able to surrender the need for control, the more self-control you're able to exert. People in flow often experience high degrees of self-control but are not distracted by needing control over things they can't influence.

6. The Loss of Self-consciousness. Why is it that when you start to worry about how you look, no matter how good you are, you lose your focus, concentration, and absorption? Anxiety about not being "good enough" will invert your external focus to an internal self-absorption and immediately stop the flow. This is why the flow experience must have clear goals and stable rules. Once these are in place, the body and mind sense that there's no relevant threat present and self-consciousness becomes unneeded and disappears.

7. The Transformation of Time. In almost all texts describing peak performance and flow is the sensation that time has either sped up or slowed down. When we're actively engaged in intense flow, time seems to slow down and gets associated with higher degrees of clarity and concentration. When recalling the experience of flow, usually after it has just ended, time is felt to have flown by.

The Joy of FlowMotion™

FlowMotion™ is a conscious, purposeful exercise done for the enjoyment and mastery of the activity itself as well as a method to actualize the intelligence, power, and playfulness of the Natural Self, your "second attention." It's the practice of inducing the physical state of flow that can't help but evoke mental, emotional, and spiritual flow. It's the alignment and focus of physical and psychic energy into a fluid, spontaneous motion that over a period of practice will transform the frozen energy of Compassion Fatigue into the fluid, living energy of flow. FlowMotion™ transforms Compassion Fatigue in several ways.

1. Physically. On the most basic, real, and tangible level, FlowMotion™ is the practice of physical flow. Compassion Fatigue is physical freezing. The body becomes brittle, fragile, the immune system compromised. FlowMotion™ transforms chronic tightness and restriction of movement into smooth, fluid movement that's coordinated and in harmony with breathing. Body awareness is increased, as is the enjoyment of *being in* the body.

2. Emotionally. When your physical body begins to break out of its rigid inflexibility, so too will your emotional "body." As we discovered earlier in the work of Candace Pert, emotions are conducted and felt in the body. The most direct and immediate route to positively influencing your emotions is to positively influence your body. By routinely practicing invigorating, energizing, and flowing movement, you will immediately and positively impact your emotions.

3. Mentally. The practice of aligning attention and intention is invaluable when developing higher levels of focus and concentration. FlowMotion™ is an intensely mental as well as physical discipline. Engaging your creative imagination to visualize, sense, and feel specific body-mind states develops focus and concentration in the service of progressive enjoyment. The better you get at focusing, visualizing, and concentrating on the release of stagnant frozen energy and the absorption of fresh, living invigorating energy, the more enjoyment you experience. And, because your visualization

---

[2] Daniel Goleman, *Emotional Intelligence,* page 92

is done in concert with smooth, flowing physical movements and full, conscious breathing, the images of your visualization will be recorded in the body as a very real, physical enjoyment that accumulates with continuous practice.

4. Spiritually. Each of us has a part to ourselves that's naturally powerful, wise, and playful, that part that I described before as the Natural Self. It's the self without image or form, belief or bias. It's the essence of self within the self, both within the center of the being and the periphery of the body. It's at the same time within the lungs and in the air that escapes the lungs, the essence of movement and the movement itself. The Natural Self is the basis of true perception, natural movement, spontaneous coordination, and dynamic balance, moving and being moved. It's the center of breath, breathing and being breathed. The Natural Self is free of the constraints of thinking, yet remains the basis of creative thought, it's free of preconception, free of desire and fear, free of time and space. FlowMotion™ invites the Natural Self to play.

FlowMotion™ is the spontaneous expression of the Natural Self in fluid, continuous motion and harmony with conscious breathing and visualization that energizes your body and emotions, focusing your mind and harmonizing your spirit with universal Energy in *MOTION*. FlowMotion™ begins with the conscious intent to surrender individual, ego-will to the dancing, flowing, playful, energy of the Natural Self.

The Form

The Form seems to just happen by itself, drifting along automatically, powered by some outside force. It does not appear as if you are making yourself move; you feel as if the Form were taking place without your conscious intent. Your attention is not standing apart from your body, directing your actions, but is flowing along with the momentum.

— Bob Klein, *Movements of Magic,* page 12

In Tai Chi and Gung Fu forms are a series of pre-determined movements done both as a way to practice and for the enjoyment

---

The Form seems to just happen by itself, drifting along automatically, powered by some outside force.

— Bob Klein, *Movements of Magic,* page 12

of the movement. The form, when given full attention, begins to take on a life of its own. When your body becomes strong and resilient enough to practice form for extended periods of time, you'll truly feel as though the form has its own center of energy and intelligence.

In some ways, FlowMotion™ can be considered as a type of "flow-form" that begins with the repetition of specific movements in combination with various styles, intensities, and rhythms of breath and motion and then progresses toward free, spontaneous expression of the Natural Self through the unpredicted movement of free-form.

Each breathing movement, relief, awareness, acceptance, and transformation, are both part of the whole of FlowMotion™ as well as complete movements in themselves. By practicing these movements, you will have begun to form some strength and resilience in your legs and back, some coordination between hands, feet, arms, and legs in harmony with conscious breathing. You'll be developing focused intention and attention with the ability to engage your creative imagination in conscious visualization.

The way in which you approach doing the form is as important as doing the form itself. What you may have already discovered by practicing the individual movements is the importance of just getting started. Because these movements are easy to learn and do, it's simple to just get out of bed in the morning, go to a specific room in your house or apartment that's designed and decorated to increase your flow of positive energy, and start doing Breath of Relief. If you're adventurous, keep a journal of your experiences. Even when you're not really feeling like doing any movement at all, if you give your body just 30 seconds of FlowMotion™, you'll immediately begin to feel more awake, alive, and energetic. That's really all it takes. Once you get moving, the natural enjoyment of the movement will begin to take over and you'll want to keep moving.

By far the best time to do FlowMotion™ is in the morning just after you get up. Give yourself just a few minutes of extra time. Approach the practice of FlowMotion™ consciously and with the specific intent to immerse yourself in the flow of the movement and the energy of conscious breathing. Look for opportunities to develop, nourish, internalize, and actualize as much vital energy and awareness as you can absorb.

The other thing to keep in mind is this: each time you can begin your day with free-flowing movement, you're physically, emotionally, mentally, and spiritually absorbing, attuning, and accumulating the fluid, expressive energy of flow. Each moment of your time and each quantum of your energy that you invest into FlowMotion™ will result in an energy bank account that may ultimately "buy" you more time.

Primarily FlowMotion™ should be done for the enjoyment of doing it. Your body-mind naturally craves flowing movement. The more you surrender yourself to this natural craving, the more you can feel the energy inside surging, dancing, and flowing.

When practicing FlowMotion™ be very patient with yourself. Even these simple motions can become difficult if you try too hard, make them too complicated, or read too much into them. Listen to your body and follow its intuition. As important as getting the specific movements, breaths, and visualizations to flow together in harmony is your constantly developing ability to "look and listen" to your body-mind intuition and your Natural Self.

I've artificially divided FlowMotion™ into four movements. Keep in mind that these are artificial separations because the whole movement is done in fluid unison. The separations are to be used as nothing more than markers. To let you get more of a sense of the fluid connectedness of each motion, I've included more focused, whole-body-flow version at the end of this chapter.

Be sure to read Chapters 11 and 12 together. Right after you finish the FlowMotion™ movements described in this chapter, you'll transition immediately into the energy stance and closing described in Chapter 12.

The Stance

Begin the FlowMotion™ form by taking the Horse Stance: your feet a bit wider than shoulder width apart with knees slightly bent, back straight, toes pointing out just slightly to the left and right. Hold your hands in front of you as though you were holding a large beach ball out from your body. Your hands should be about 18 inches apart from each other, elbows slightly bent, palms facing toward each other and turned slightly down. Allow your arms and shoulders to relax. Relax your neck and straighten your back as you allow your core center to "float."

Now direct your attention to the ground and *into* the ground, allowing your awareness to expand to include sensing the energy that's literally absorbed into, and radiating out from, the earth. Sense your personal connection with the earth and with this energy. Consciously engage your creative imagination to extend and attune your awareness to sense the living, flowing, energy that's constantly radiating up from the earth. Visualize and imaginatively sense this energy penetrating the soles of your feet and extending through your knees and thighs to your core.

Now allow your awareness to feel the structure and support of your back and your spine, particularly your lower back. Place your attention into your lower back as you continue to breathe energy through your core. Allow your awareness to surround and penetrate any frozen energy that has taken root as muscle memory. Breathe energy and awareness into your lower back to soothe and circulate the *Energy* in *MOTION*.

Bring your attention to your hands, arms, shoulders, and neck. Feel the latent energy in your hands, arms, and shoulders as you hold them out. Breathe a deep breath and consciously relax your shoulders by letting them drop as you exhale. Allow your shoulders to gently, and just slightly, roll forward.

Just before you begin the first motion, allow your attention to scan and connect all parts of your body-mind into a fluid, coherent sense of self. This stance is your beginning position and all movement flows from it. It's also a "body-statement" that expresses your sense of self-coherence and consolidation. Sense the natural solidity and balance that's inherent in this living body position, the wide base and solid connection to the earth, the lowered center of gravity and redirection of your attention, from your head-ego to your core-Natural Self. Begin the first movement from deep within your core center.

First Movement

Begin this first FlowMotion™ movement by discharging any old, residual breath that may still be in your lungs by consciously squeezing in your lower abdomen and pushing out all of your breath in a steady stream. Push out your breath until you can feel the natural pull of your lungs to fill the vacuum you just created.

As you draw in a steady, deep breath from your diaphragm to a count of four, imagine that your awareness is actually in your core. Visualize that you're "pulling" energy up and in from the earth and air, through the silver dollar size energy portals in the middle of your soles and palms as well as through your lungs. Sense and feel your body-mind drinking in this living, aware energy.

As your hands are breathed in toward your heart, sense the feeling of an opening in the palms that is "drinking in" energy from the environment around you. As you breathe in fresh, revitalizing oxygen, begin to allow your center of gravity to gently sink in an effortless, floating motion. Rather than gravity being felt as a force that keeps you down, experience its energy as a force that connects you with the earth. Rather than fighting the pull of gravity, float on its energy.

As your center sinks down, imagine that you are drawing energy up through your feet, ankles and thighs into your core. Coordinate your movements so that your hands and arms are contracting toward your heart center as your knees are slowly bending to the force of gravity lowering your core toward the ground.

Open your core and your heart to living, intelligent, nurturing, connecting energy as you breathe in fully from your diaphragm. Sense, feel, and visualize this energy being drawn up from the ground through your feet and in through your palms as your legs and arms contract in harmony.

As you bend your knees and lower your center of gravity, pay attention to your back and your balance. Hold your back with a little arch so that your pelvis is slightly tilted forward. Allow gravity to do its work; you just supply the brakes. Allow gravity to slowly, smoothly and gently pull you toward the ground.

As you pull your hands toward your chest, feel a vibrant, nurturing energy being pulled with your palms into your heart center. As you fill your lungs with fresh oxygen, imagine that you're also filling your heart with fresh, vibrant energy; allow this energy to circulate through your heart center. Visualize this *Energy* in *MOTION* freeing old, stagnant freeze-energy that has taken root as body memory.

When you reach that place where you can't comfortably bend your legs and knees, allow your center to slow its momentum. Your hands are pulled in toward your chest. Your lungs are filled with fresh oxygen and your core and your heart are charged with energy.

Just as the momentum in your legs begins to transition from down to up, allow your legs to gently, slowly, and smoothly bounce during the space that your in-breath is transitioning to out-breath. As you complete the gentle bounce, begin breathing out as you sense the momentum in your legs pushing you up. As much as you can, "ride" on the momentum created by the downward motion. Convert the downward energy into upward energy by "bouncing" on the ball of energy that has been created by your breath, energy, and motion.

Breathe out slowly, smoothly, and continuously to a count of five. Breathe energy and awareness from your core into your thighs, knees, ankles, and back as you begin to stand. Use minimal muscle energy to lift your body upwards. Open yourself to a different kind of energy created and directed by breath, energy, and motion. It's the energy of effortless effort.

Breathe energy-awareness from your heart center into your hands as your arms begin to effortlessly straighten your elbows. Allow this energy-awareness to propel your arms and hands forward with as little consciously directed effort on your part as possible.

As your legs and arms straighten in harmony with the smooth releasing of your breath, imagine that your center of gravity is actually floating upward from the outward force of your breath. Allow your body to mirror the outward flow of breath and expansion of your energy.

Allow your arms to continue straightening in harmony with your out-breath. Imagine you're breathing energy from your heart-center into your palms. Sense and feel this warm, vibrating energy tingling your palms and penetrating the silver dollar energy vortices in the centers as your hands extend, palms out, elbows just slightly bent.

As your breath empties out completely, allow your body to come to a standing position, with a slight bend in your knees. Your arms should be fully extended with a slight bend in your elbows, hands about six inches apart, palms facing outward. Shoulders and elbows are relaxed and held loosely.

In the moment of transition between out-breath and in-breath, upward–outward motion and inward-downward motion, extending and recovering energy, immerse yourself in a state of suspended attention. As you allow your mind to suspend its activity, and while your body is suspended in motion, suspend your sense of time; spend a second of eternity in that sweet place of pure awareness and clarity.

Second Movement

Consciously pull in a deep, full, even breath from your diaphragm to a count of four as you allow your hands and arms to mirror your breath. As lightly, smoothly, and fluidly as you can, pull your hands in toward your heart in harmony and coordination with your breath.

Allow the energy that was extended in front of you to smoothly and fluidly recoil into an inward motion as it springs back through the silver dollar energy spots in the centers of your palms. Sense this energy being pulled back into your core through your palms as though a vacuum had been created by its upward-outward extension. As your diaphragm opens to draw in oxygen, allow your awareness to be in your feet as you draw energy with them from the earth.

This time, as you begin to bend your knees, hold just a little tension in your legs as you consciously squeeze your thigh muscles in harmony with lowering your center of gravity to the ground. Squeeze just hard enough to feel the muscles move; don't inhibit the movement. When you squeeze your legs like this, it serves as a way to store energy in the muscle.

As your hands naturally and smoothly pull in toward your heart-center with the rebound of energy, allow them to ride on the waves of momentum returning to your core. Imagine and visualize waves of pure, conscious energy rebounding up from the earth, in from your palms, and synergizing in your core.

Allow the momentum in your legs to begin to transition from down to up as your legs begin to gently, slowly, and smoothly bounce during the space that your in-breath is changing to out-breath. During this point of transition from down to up, in to out, inhale to exhale, there's a sweet moment of weightlessness and timelessness as breath, energy, motion, and momentum are suspended.

As you complete the gentle bounce, begin breathing out, sensing the momentum in your legs pushing you up. As much as you can, "ride" on the momentum created by the downward motion. Convert the downward energy into upward energy by "bouncing" on the ball of energy created by your breath, energy, and motion. Allow the incoming momentum of energy in your palms to convert to an upward motion by allowing your elbows to flare out to the right and left just as you begin the bounce of upward energy. As your downward energy bounces into an upward force, allow your hands to mirror the bouncing movement to begin their upward momentum.

From your core, form an intention to extend your breath, awareness, energy, and motion through the center of your body and out the palms of your hands in a single, seamless motion. Visualize with your mind and sense in your body the smooth, flowing, coordinated movement, lifting, standing, and extending as your breath is released to a count of four.

Consciously push your breath out from your diaphragm and control the flow of oxygen by constricting the muscles around your throat and vocal chords into a voiceless "Ahhh…." As you breathe out, allow your legs to release their stored-up kinetic energy and begin to stand. Remember to keep your back straight so that your center hovers and there's a straight line up from your core to your head. Slowly release your breath and allow your knees and legs to straighten as if they had a mind of their own. Allow your body to follow your core intent to extend energy and awareness up through the palms of your hands into the vortex of pure, positive, aware energy just above your head.

In synchronization with your legs and breath, give over to the feeling or sensation that your hands have an awareness of their own. Allow the awareness you feel in your core to extend and merge with the awareness you sense in your palms as your hands begin their upward motion. Springing on the momentum stored as

kinetic energy in your legs, allow your arms and hands to ride on this cushion of energy as it extends upward.

Follow your hands with your eyes. Notice how your hands seem to "scoop" energy from your heart center and carry it up toward the vortex that has manifested above your head and that attracts your hands and body with its magnetic pull. As your hands reach eye level, notice that they begin to naturally rotate from palms facing inward to palms facing upward. Allow this transition to occur naturally, effortlessly.

As your eyes continue to follow your hands up, again become aware of the muscle tension in the back of your neck. Just notice the tension and allow your awareness to enter into the muscle itself. As you discharge the last of your breath, extend your palms up as far as they will comfortably go with a slight bend in your elbows. As you stretch to extend your palms, allow your lower back to arch and your head to lean slightly back.

Visualize vital, flowing Qi energy being pulled up from the earth, into your core with your breath, through your backbone and spine, into the back of your neck, and finally out the palms of your hands

into the vortex, circulating, transforming, and revitalizing frozen energy into flow energy.

Third Movement

You're now standing firmly rooted to the ground, your body in alignment, with your knees and elbows slightly bent, reaching toward the sky, palms facing upward. Your head, neck, and back are all slightly arched, your eyes are focused on your hands, your lungs are empty. Allow yourself to be completely empty for just a couple of seconds.

As the vacuum of emptiness easily and naturally transforms to the inhalation of breath, allow your outward focused energy to begin to collapse inward. Just as exhaling your breath created a wave of air out away from you that will eventually transform and return to the source, your Qi energy also travels out to yo-yo back.

Begin to take in a long, slow, deep breath from your diaphragm to a count of four and visualize that you're reaching up, into a vortex of pure awareness-energy. Imagine that you're pulling in pure awareness-energy through your palms as you begin to draw in your hands.

Continue to draw your hands down toward your center and breathe in slowly and smoothly from your diaphragm. Engage your creative imagination and visualize that your palms are actually drinking in living, flowing awareness-energy being drawn in toward your core. Imagine that you're breathing this awareness-energy into every cell in your body.

As you bend your elbows to pull down your hands, also bend your knees and slowly, gently, lower your center of gravity. Be sure to keep your back straight rather than bending forward. Be careful not to strain your back or knees.

Allow your core to float effortlessly toward the earth and continue to breathe in fully from your diaphragm. Extend and connect your awareness, from your palms pulling and drinking in revitalizing energy and awareness, to your incoming breath circulating that energy-awareness to your core.

Continue to pull your hands toward your center as your draw in energy through your palms and notice how they effortlessly rotate inward so they face each other by the time they're eye-level. Also be aware of the sensation in the back of your neck as your head moves with your eyes, following your hands. Can you feel the release of tension?

Follow your hands with your eyes as they're pulled down toward your chest and heart by the same energy that floats your center. Your lungs are beginning to feel full with oxygen.

As your hands continue their downward path, your legs and knees also continue to bend, slowly, smoothly lowering your center of gravity toward the earth to the extent you're comfortable. Allow your center of gravity to be pulled closer to the earth and keep your back straight so that you don't bend forward with the motion. Allow the full weight of your body to be supported by your legs and suspended in your center.

Visualize that you're actually pulling, breathing, and circulating this energy from the top of your head, down the midline of your body, into your heart. Sense this energy connecting and circulating between your heart and your core, your core and the earth. With a single, fluid motion of your hands, draw in and circulate vital awareness energy through your entire body and into your core where it collects and compresses.

As the momentum of your downward motion glides to a halt and begins to transition to an upward motion, allow your center a little bounce as downward-inward-absorbing motion is being transformed to an upward-outward-expressive motion.

Just as your center lightly bounces up, allow the downward motion of your hands seamlessly to transform into an upward crossing motion so that your wrists are lightly touching in the shape of an X; your right hand is now your left and your left is now your right. Your upward bouncing motion has reached its apex and your lungs are completely full of oxygen and energy.

Pause for just a second in fullness; your knees and legs are crouched, full of energy and momentum, your back is straight, your lungs are full of oxygen and energy, and your hands and arms are crossed at the wrists. Sense deep in your core the convergence and compression of vital, living, intelligent energy that has been pulled in from the earth through your feet and the vortex through your palms. When the momentum of the energy stored in your body reaches the turning point, allow that energy to transform into an expressive energy as you begin to release your breath.

Exhale your breath with controlled force as you activate the muscles of your arms and legs when springing back to a standing position. Breathe out in a controlled, intense stream of oxygen to a count of three as you straighten your arms and legs. Consciously tighten your quadriceps and slowly push the center of your body up with your legs. Breathe energy into your arms as you allow the energy in your hands to be released and transformed into outward, expressive movement. As you begin to stand up, breathe oxygen and energy in and through your hands as they reverse direction and begin to travel away from each other.

Feed your expressive, outwardly directed energy and motion with your breath and from your core, continuing to keep some part of your attention-energy focused there. Even as you feed your

motions with breath and energy, imagine that you're extending your core energy and awareness into your body by consciously "feeding" and nourishing your sense of self with breath and energy. Continue to consciously breathe awareness, energy, and motion from your core through your legs, arms, and hands as you push your energy and awareness through the silver dollar spots in the middle of your palms. As your hands reach the point in their outward movement where your palms are again facing out to the left and right as though you were about to push on pillars to either side of you, tighten the muscles in your arms and forcefully exhale the remainder of your breath through your throat with a silent "Hahhhh…."

As the last of your breath rushes out, release the tension completely from your arms and legs and allow the Qi energy to rush out the silver dollar spots in your palms. As you suddenly and consciously relax your physical tension, you also release Qi energy that was stored in your body and breath.

Extend your Qi energy through your palms, out away from your body, and into the external environment by consciously sensing and imagining an almost sticky, plasma-like energy extending through the silver dollar spots in the middle of your palms. Imagine and sense in your hands this electric-elastic energy shooting out your palms in concert with the final thrust of your breath and motion. Continue to imaginatively follow this energy. Imagine that the initial outward thrust of energy doesn't actually dispel and weaken, but transforms and attracts energy with a similar positive charge returning back through your palms as your diaphragm creates the vacuum to draw in breath and energy.

Fourth Motion

Assist your intuition and imaginatively visualize the energy extended out through your palms on the exhale being pulled back in with even more energy as you inhale a long, slow, deep, even breath from your diaphragm to a count of five. As you pull in your hands and arms with a scooping motion, allow your center to mirror your hands. On the downward part of the scoop your center sinks, on the upward part your center rises.

Visualize that you're "scooping" energy with your hands in harmony with your in-breath. When your hands have scooped "up" as far as the momentum will take the motion, and you've fully extended your legs and center, feel a "sloshing" of plasma energy in your core. For just a brief moment, absorb the fullness of life-giving energy surging in your core.

As you feel upward moving energy and momentum naturally begin to convert to downward, expressive *Energy* in *MOTION,* allow your hands to surrender to the force of gravity and fall back toward the earth. As your hands and energy flow back down, continue to mirror your hands with your center and allow it to sink in harmony with the movement of your hands.

Continue to breath in as your hands gain momentum in their falling motion and allow them to swing out in a loop to the right and left. As your hands follow the upward arc set by your elbows, you can sense the connection of energy between your core and your hands, as your palms pull this plasma energy into the shape of an upward arc.

Begin to straighten your knees with your back remaining straight and aligned. As your hands continue their upward arc, imagine this pulling motion drawing energy up from your core through the center of your body while remaining connected to the energy vortices in your palms. This drawing motion also feels as though you're pulling your weight or gravity up through your center so that you actually feel lighter. Your knees straighten automatically and harmoniously with the movement.

As your elbows reach chest level and your lungs are nearly full of oxygen and energy, allow your hands to naturally rotate with the movement of your arms as they begin to reach rather than pull upwards. Allow your hands to begin to reach in an upward arcing motion as your palms simultaneously begin to face each other, fingers held loosely and slightly apart from each other.

As you pull energy up from your core through the middle of your body into your heart center, feel it collect in your hands. It will feel as though your hands actually have more gravity and weight. As your hands begin to reach in harmony over your head, allow them to be pulled toward each other, palm to palm as if they were magnetically drawn. Experience the upward flow of energy from your heart-center to the crown of your head, as your lungs are full and nourished with fresh, vital, oxygen and energy.

At the point where your hands are suspended over your head, palm to palm about six inches apart, your legs are fully extended with a slight bend in your knees, your back is slightly arched, and your lungs are full of oxygen, allow your in-breath to seamlessly transition to out-breath. Suspend your attention and allow your awareness to hover at this transition point from fullness back to emptiness.

Allow the breath to flow out from your throat through your mouth in a voiceless "Ahhh…" sound to a count of four. Control the volume and intensity of your oxygen by squeezing those inner throat muscles that restrict the passage of air through your larynx. With the absence of physical tension or force, begin to intensely pull your palms straight down the center of your forehead. Continue to pull your hands down the centerline of your head and face as you lower your center of gravity by bending your knees. As you bend your knees, visualize that you're "collapsing in" toward your center. Allow the downward pull of your hands, energy, and the earth to pull your center of gravity down and in while continuing to keep your back straight and aligned.

Begin to follow your hands with your eyes. As your hands descend past your face to heart level, feel the stretching in the back of your neck with the movement of your head. Consciously allow the muscles in the back of your neck and shoulders to stretch and relax as your eyes continue to follow your hands.

By the time your hands have reached your abdomen, your knees should be fully bent and your center as low to the ground as it can comfortably be. Your pulling down hand-arm movement will also be at a point of transition, from pulling to pushing. As your hands become parallel with your elbows and are extended just out from your abdomen, your pulling down motion will smoothly and seamlessly transition into a pushing down motion. Begin to straighten your knees as you push your palms and energy toward the earth. Continue pushing your hands down, palms facing the earth as you straighten your legs to a standing position. Visualize that you're actually transmitting energy from your palms to the earth and from the earth to your palms as they lightly bounce down and then up just as you complete your out-breath.

When you return to the original stance, take a second to just look and listen; can you sense the earth calling to you again? If you can, allow your breath, energy, and motion to slowly, smoothly, and seamlessly transition into allowing your knees to bend as you take in another slow, deep, even breath from your diaphragm.

Continuous FlowMotion™

Bending your knees and pulling in your arms, allow yourself to sink slowly toward the ground as you breathe in fully from your diaphragm. Visualize drawing strength and energy from the earth through your feet and legs, filling every muscle, nerve, and tissue in your body with its life giving Qi. When you've allowed your body to sink as comfortably as it can with your spine straight and aligned, allow yourself to feel a little cushion of energy that softly springs you up as the momentum of your Qi begins to shift from down to up.

As your legs and arms begin to slowly and effortlessly straighten out, imagine that you're actually being pulled up, as much as pushed up, by your legs. As you breathe out in harmony with your motion, imagine that your breath is exhaling old, stagnant, frozen energy that has been freed and cleared from your body and mind. Imagine all of that old energy being discharged as your breath leaves your body.

With continual, fluid motion and consciousness, begin again to draw your hands in toward you as you bend your elbows and knees. Breathe oxygen and energy deeply into your lungs and your center. Use your imagination to visualize energy being pulled into your core through your palms. As you continue to fill your lungs with this slow, deep breath, imagine this breath as energy invigorating every cell in your body.

As you gently bounce up, look upwards as though toward the heavens. Use your full powers of visualization to see and feel just above you your brightest, clearest experience of inspiration, creativity, and harmony.

Begin to reach up to touch this positive, intelligent energy. As you stand up, allow both hands to reach in harmony as if they were being pulled by a force over your head. As you exhale, standing completely straight with arms and hands outstretched, imagine you're emptying out all of your old, stagnant energy.

As you breathe in, pull your hands, breath, and energy in toward your center. Allow your right and left hand to cross in front of you as though they were crossing swords. As you begin to straighten your body to "push" your energy through your arms and hands, coordinate your breath to exhale just as you push your hands and energy to the right and the left.

Exhale fully, deeply, and slowly. Your oxygen is the carrier of energy; allow it to circulate and flow freely through your entire body, bringing life and vitality. Allow your hands and arms to flow out with the expansion and expression of your breath and energy. Continue to flow with your breath, energy, and motion. In practice, all movements are continuous and fluid. There is no real beginning or ending. Regardless of the pace, force or intensity of the energy, the movements are continually flowing like water from one container to the next.

Pull your hands into the center of your chest, as though they were around a large beach ball of energy that you're holding. Feel this fluid energy circulate through your body as you draw a large circle with both hands out, up, and over your head, as though you were pouring this energy over the top of you, allowing it to flow over, in, and around your very being.

As your hands flow down over the top of your head to your waist, straighten your elbows and knees, coming to a standing position with your legs bent, back straight, arms at your side, your breath flowing out leaving you with the physical, emotional, and mental experience of harmony and clarity.

Just as you come to a standing position, returning to the original stance, allow your attention to drop inside your core. Can you sense another invitation in the shape of a forming vacuum? If you can, once again begin to bend your knees, pull in your arms, and allow yourself to sink slowly toward the ground as you breathe in fully from your diaphragm....

Practicing FlowMotion™

When you first begin to practice FlowMotion™ the movements may seem a little mechanical and stiff, your body out of alignment and out of rhythm with your breathing. This is completely natural and fine. Allow and accept the initial disorganization and disconnection your body may feel; many people feel initially uncomfortable being conscious in their bodies. The tendency is to get an idea or picture in your head of how you're "supposed" to look based on what you see on the DVD. What you see on the DVD is my body's interpretation and expression of flow; your body's interpretation is quite likely to be different than mine.

FlowMotion™ is a conscious, creative expression of your Natural Self. It's not the mechanical repetition of someone else's vision. The joy and the power of FlowMotion™ come from its creative re-invention each time you do each and every movement. This requires that you become internally silent and receptive to the energy flow that's already there. Rather than your ego trying to dictate to your Natural Self how you should look, surrender your movement to the music that's playing in your Natural Self.

When you first begin practicing FlowMotion™ it's natural to concentrate on just getting the basic movements, sense of balance, and breathing coordinated together. Don't worry so much about energy and visualization. Pay more attention to your center of balance, keeping your back straight, and pulling in your hands as you bend your knees. You will also need to get a sense of just how much you can bend your knees.

It's a good idea to begin with just a slight bend in your knees as you breathe in with a very shallow dip in the transition between breaths, slowly straightening your knees as you exhale. If that feels comfortable, smoothly transition into bending your knees a little deeper on the next breath.

As you begin to get a sense of timing and rhythm to your movements so that you're breathing in harmony with the inflow and outflow of your motions, allow your attention to focus more on the smoothness and connection between each individual motion. Sense that every motion is comprised of many smaller movements that are all connected together. As you move, focus your attention into each and every portion of the movement so that you can sense the continuity in and between each motion.

When your individual movements feel more connected, you'll begin to sense the connection between the individual parts of your body. Rather than experiencing your right hand and left foot as disconnected entities, you'll begin to feel them connected, in harmony, so that when the right hand moves, the left foot immediately knows it and responds.

With practice, your legs and back will become stronger and more resilient. This will simply take time. It's necessary to gain this strength and resilience so that your body can tolerate the energy that you're generating and navigating through it. It will also allow you to experience certain energy releases, patterns, and rhythms that weren't available with shorter practice.

The longer you can flow, the more your body learns. The difference between doing FlowMotion™ for 5 minutes and 15 minutes is a quantum leap! From my experience so far (even I'm still learning and experimenting), the more you're able to surrender your body movement and awareness over to the energy generated by the motion, the deeper, more absorbed and focused your attention becomes. The less it is "you" doing the movement, the more you allow the movement to "do you," the greater the sense of flow and enjoyment.

If you do FlowMotion™ for the enjoyment and mastery of the movement, you'll be continually led to new rhythms, tempos, and variations of the movement. Allow yourself to be led by your core, your intuition, and your Natural Self to the next level of transformation. Each level of transformation is expressed in different nuances of the form that spontaneously present themselves to your body-mind awareness when you're ready to make the transition.

Be sure to read Chapter 12 next to learn the Energy Stance and Closing before practicing FlowMotion™. These last two stances are critical to discharging, re-charging, releasing, and transforming the energy that has been activated by the movements.

Chapter Twelve:

Transforming Energy in MOTION

Through transformation, the nervous system regains
its capacity for self-regulation. Our emotions begin
to lift us up rather than bring us down. They propel us
into the exhilarating ability to soar and fly, giving us a
more complete view of our place in nature.

— Peter Levine, *Waking the Tiger: Healing Trauma*, page 103

Introduction

When learning Qigong from Master Yong, I didn't fully realize the significance of the last two stances, the energy stance and the closing, until years later when sharing Qigong with a Chinese physician I consulted after moving back from Singapore. It wasn't until I demonstrated Qigong fully, including the energy stance with all of its vibrating and shaking and the closing, that he said, "Ah, so you do know Qigong."

It was right then and there I remembered that Sifu would always insist on completing the energy stance and closing as the last Qigong movements before meditating. As usual, he would never explain why and I never asked.

What I would learn years later from reviewing the current research on Post Traumatic Stress Disorder (PTSD) and Compassion Fatigue was that the shaking and trembling that accompanies holding your body position in a precise stance after practicing Qigong or FlowMotion™ is the discharging and transforming of the "frozen residue" of traumatic stress energy that has been trapped in your body as chronic tightness or numbness. The shaking and trembling in your legs is the physical manifestation of releasing trauma. It's essential to the completion of the exercise to discharge and then close your energy center by placing both hands over the Tan T'ien and then breathing long, slow, deep, even breaths from the diaphragm.

Energy transformation is an actual physical/emotional process that is at times very difficult to describe in words. When you take the energy stance and consciously focus your attention inwards toward the vortex of the traumatic energy that you "sense-feel" in your body, you'll begin to notice your knees and legs "wanting" to shake and tremble. If you allow yourself to surrender to this movement, rather than tighten and fight it, you'll find that the trembling and shaking begins to take on a life of its own.

As you consciously relax into the movement, you may find the trembling will change its intensity, frequency, rhythm, even direction. At times your knees can shake, jump, or rotate. It appears at first as if all the action happens in the legs and knees but if you stay with the experience, the vibration can travel from your legs into your core and even into your back, neck, and shoulders.

As you allow the vibration to take on its own form, energy, and frequency, you may begin to sense that as the traumatic stress energy begins to discharge, a new, invigorating, life-sustaining vortex of energy begins to emerge. The process of traumatic stress energy discharging and dissipating and being transformed into life-sustaining energy is what Dr. Levine in *Waking the Tiger: Healing Trauma* calls renegotiation: "By beginning with the healing vortex," he writes, "we pick up the support and resources needed to successfully negotiate the trauma vortex. By moving between these vortices, we release the tightly bound energies at their cores — as if they were being unwound. We move toward their centers and their energies are released; the vortices break up, dissolve, and are integrated back into the mainstream. This is renegotiation."[1]

When you first begin FlowMotion™ you may or may not get the vibration when taking the energy stance. This may be because you're out of alignment when holding the stance, or you don't yet have the strength and resiliency in your legs and back to do FlowMotion™ continuously for 5 to 10 minutes. This is why it's so important to practice each individual breath exercise until you're comfortable with the movement and your back and legs begin to develop the strength and resiliency necessary to sustain continuous motion. The continual practice of FlowMotion™ will strengthen your legs and back to give you a firm foundation and deep connection to the earth.

The last movement, the closing, is done after the vibration in your body has settled and stopped and you instinctively feel ready to close off the energy flow from your Tan T'ien. This is not the same thing as stopping the energy flow. It's simply holding the energy inside to circulate.

The closing, which ends by placing both hands over your Tan T'ien or core, directs the energy centers in your palms toward the large energy vortex in your core, allowing the energy to settle and circulate. It is also preventing a major energy leak from your core. In fact, many of our large energy leaks can often be traced back to continual tension or a frozen absence of awareness in the gut.

---

[1] Peter Levine, *Waking the Tiger: Healing Trauma,* page 199

The Energy Stance

When you first begin doing FlowMotion™ it may be difficult to do even more than five repetitions. You can immediately feel the weakness in your knees, legs, and back that's a result of having "starved" your lower body from needed attention. The less conscious attention you feed a part of your body-mind, the less solid, coherent, and powerful you are in that part of your body. Much of your physical strength and resilience is actually comprised of focused attention energy.

Do your best to let go of the temptation to try to do too much too quickly. If you can begin to feel the flow of energy after doing five repetitions of FlowMotion™, take a moment to absorb the feeling of flow and allow your attention to become attuned to it. If you're not feeling too sore or too weak, try another three. If you begin to feel yourself trying too hard and straining too much so that you're not feeling a sense of flow and enjoyment, then it's time to stop and take the energy stance.

When you finish the last exhale of your final FlowMotion™ movement and your hands are suspended in front of you as though they were holding onto a large beach ball, allow yourself to take two or three long, deep breaths. Allow the momentum of all your breathing, movement, and energy to slowly settle.

When you feel an inner stillness beginning to form, draw both feet closer together so that they're right at about shoulder width apart. Turn your toes inward so that they're slightly pointed toward each other. This will cause your knees to bend inward. Your center of gravity will be leaning just slightly forward while remaining suspended.

Continue to keep a small arch in the small of your back and allow your weight to focus in your legs as you slightly lower your center of gravity. As you gently bend your knees, they should bend inward, closer to each other. You should simultaneously feel the tug in your quadriceps, the large muscles in your legs, as they squeeze harder to float your center.

As your feet settle into the energy stance, bring your attention to your hands and arms. Allow your hands to float in front of you by turning your palms toward the ground and expanding the space between your hands. Continue to keep your elbows bent so that your arms almost form a circle. Let your fingers and thumbs relax so there's space between each of them.

Relax your shoulders and let your elbows slightly droop. Be especially conscious of the muscles that connect your neck and shoulders and allow them to loosen and relax. Slightly bounce your knees to let your weight adjust and find its natural center as you breathe naturally without effort or strain. Allow your breath to breathe itself as you hold this stance.

Bring your attention to your core. What do you notice? Can you feel all the different parts of your body, your hands, elbows, arms, shoulders, neck, back, legs, knees, and feet connected together by your breath and awareness? Allow your attention to centralize in your core and to radiate out to every part of your body, connecting each part together. Can you get a sense or glimpse of wholeness and unity existing side by side with separation and individuality?

As you focus your awareness in your core, can you feel the pressure in your legs? Because your legs are tired from the FlowMotion™ movements and are held in a position that focuses the weight of your body onto your quadriceps, you may begin to feel a sense of weakness or shakiness in your knees. Do you feel "weak in the knees?"

For many of us, Compassion Fatigue is felt as an absence of strength, resiliency and awareness in our legs, our base upon which we stand. We habitually and unconsciously withhold our energy and attention from this part of the body. Being grounded is to actually feel yourself in your legs. It's to have a solid relationship with the earth.

Can you feel your knees wanting to shake? Do you sense a slight tremulousness in your legs? If you don't yet sense the energy in your legs, slightly and very slowly straighten your knees until you feel them jump or tremble. The moment you feel the trembling, allow yourself to sense the energy in your legs and give them permission to discharge that energy. Relax into the sense of "weakness" in your legs and knees rather than fight it.

If your knees don't jump or tremble as you slowly straighten your legs, don't worry about it. It can take some time to develop enough resilience in your legs to absorb enough energy from the FlowMotion™ movements to be discharged in the energy stance. Continue to try the stance each time you finish the movements.

If your knees do tremble or jump, hold them in that same position. Relax and allow your weight to concentrate in your knees and quadriceps. As you allow the trembling to manifest, enter into the trembling motion itself with your awareness. What do you notice?

Do you notice the trembling begin to take the shape of shaking back and forth? How about shaking your knees round and round in a circle? What about up and down shaking, almost a jolting? As much as you're able, surrender the need to control your physical responses and allow your body to express and release the energy stored in it.

Allow your legs to shake and tremble in whatever motion, direction, and rhythm they choose. Trust you natural body intelligence. When you begin to feel the trembling lessen, allow your knees to slowly and slightly straighten until you feel the trembling again. Allow the trembling to express and exhaust itself as before. Continue to straighten your knees in this way until you are standing straight.

Over time, as you train your attention to notice more subtle nuances of rhythm and energy patterns, you may begin to recognize traces of emotions, memories, perceptions, and thought patterns just behind or actually in the trembling energy. Because the trembling so closely resembles your body's response to trauma, your body is actually remembering trauma that has been stored as body memory, releasing and "renegotiating" the trauma.

Don't be surprised if other parts of your body begin to tremble and shake as well. You can hold trauma in many parts of your body including your neck and shoulders. I can remember times in Singapore training with other Qigong students when some of them would shake and tremble throughout their whole bodies quite vigorously. I've personally experienced trembling in my back, neck, stomach, chest, and shoulders.

Closing

When you've "renegotiated" most of your residual energy, at least for this session, your body will stop its trembling and there will be an internal sense of "enoughness," a state of feeling complete, as though a circuit had just been closed. There's no reason to do any more. There's no sense of longing for more or of having done too much. Enoughness is a state of internal balance and responsiveness. You neither feel more nor less than who you are.

When your body-mind senses enoughness, slowly and smoothly move your left foot closer to your right while beginning a full in-breath from your diaphragm to a count of three. Allow both hands to swing down to your waist. When your feet are about two feet apart from each other, allow your palms to turn as your hands begin a slow, smooth, connected upward swing over your head. Breathe consciously through the energy vortices in the centers of your palms as your hands are pulled out and up.

Imagine that your breath and hands are connected together. As your arms begin to lift your hands in an upward arc, visualize your in-breath effortlessly pulling your hands up, palms facing each other, elbows slightly extended to the left and right.

Continue to imagine that your hands and breath are connected to the Qi energy circulating inside your body and connecting you to the earth. Visualize as you pull your hands and breath up, that you're also pulling Qi up from the Earth through the energy portals in the soles of your feet. Visualize this energy being drawn into your core.

Allow your hands to continue their outward, upward movement past your chest and sense Qi energy being pulled into your heart center. As your hands begin to reach the apex of the movement, sense your Qi energy being pulled to the top of your head just as your lungs become full of fresh oxygen and energy.

Smoothly and seamlessly allow in-breath to transition to out-breath as your hands begin their downward journey, palms facing each other. Sense your Qi energy "sloshing" back down from the top of your head as you begin your out-breath. Allow your spent oxygen to escape to a count of three.

As your breath is smoothly and fluidly exhaled, pull your hands in an imaginary line down the center of your body. Sense in your palms that you're pulling Qi energy from the top of your head, through your heart center, and into your core as your hands continue their downward movement.

When your hands reach your abdomen allow them to turn and face the ground. During the last part of the movement, "push" your hands past your core and imagine that you're also pushing your Qi from your core, through your legs, and out the soles of your feet into the earth just as you push all of your breath from your diaphragm and become empty.

Without hesitation or thought, repeat the movement two more times. Each time visualize that you're smoothing and circulating energy through your entire body. On your in-breath, pull the energy from the earth through your body to the top of your head; on the out-breath push your Qi energy from the top of your head back through your heart center and core into the earth.

After three full circulations of your breath, energy, and motion, place your left hand over your Tan T'ien, and your right hand over your left. Breathe naturally.

Allow your stance to widen just a little and relax the small of your back by gently extending your pelvis. Allow your shoulders to roll forward slightly so that your chest sinks in with a protective concave around your heart center. Allow your body to take as relaxed a position as it can while you continue to breathe naturally.

Center your attention: allow it to sink from your head-ego to your center-core. Allow your awareness to mirror your breath, circulating it with your breath and energy as you breathe in. Be as receptive as you can to the energy patterns that are active in your body. Just sense and observe them.

With each breath, sense any changes in the frequency, intensity, and volume of your Qi energy. There's no right or wrong frequency; just observe. Observe the "direction" of your energy and how organized versus chaotic it is. Can you sense any emotions or body sensations associated with the energy? Do whole or fragmented images or memories surface?

If you find that your attention is drawn away by distracting thoughts or intrusive images, breathe deeply and return your attention to your breath and to your core. If you can't return your attention to your core-breath and the images, thoughts, and emotions become disturbing, discontinue the exercise. Don't feel that you have to "fight" or "beat" these feelings and images. They are, after all, a part of you. Discontinue and try again at another time.

If you're able to circulate your breath and energy, continue to do so for at least three or four minutes. You should have the feeling or sensation that you're actually holding vital energy in by placing both hands over your major energy vortex, the Tan T'ien. This will help your energy circulate and take root. Over time, as you discharge energy residue, you will also begin to accumulate and store this living and vital life energy.

Taking the First Step

Breath of Relief and the other movements that make up FlowMotion™ will help unfreeze, loosen, express, resolve and transform the frozen, rigid *Energy* in *MOTION* of Compassion Fatigue into the living, conscious, vibrant energy of flow. Each time you give your Natural Self permission to play, to spontaneously and creatively express itself through your thoughts, feelings, and actions, your perception expands and evolves to another "gate" of awareness.

We're confronted each and every day, over and over, with a choice; we can either react automatically and mindlessly to the continual barrage of stresses and trauma that is woven into the fabric of our runaway lives, or we can consciously transform our perception by renegotiating frozen fear into fluid flow.

Each morning you have the opportunity to shape your day. You can either get up the way you always do, maybe putting the snooze alarm on two or three times, waiting to the last possible moment to get out of bed, or you can try something different.

For just one week, get up 15 minutes earlier. Think about it: if waiting to the very last minute to get up could possibly make you feel significantly better, wouldn't it have done so by now? Let go of what's not working and try something new. Make an agreement with yourself to get up 15 minutes earlier where you can give yourself some (needed) undivided attention and begin with Breath of Relief. Read the chapter, do the preliminary exercises,

and watch the DVD. Each chapter is written to help give you an in-your-body sense of what it feels like to do each movement. The DVD will give you a visual model to watch and imitate. It's sometimes useful to imitate a model until you feel more connected with your body-mind.

Let your experience be what it is. Do your best not to compare it with a model of what you think it should be. Allow your attention to sink into your body when doing the movements. When your ego becomes very active and intrusive with its judgments and criticisms, simply return your attention to your breath and to the flow of energy.

Most of all, allow yourself to experience the body-enjoyment of simple, natural, fluid movement. I am always amazed at how quickly and deeply engaged in the mind-body experience of flow participants at my workshops become with just a brief demonstration of FlowMotion™. Your Natural Self really does want to flow. If you'll commit just 15 minutes in the morning for the next week and give your body-mind complete permission to become fully immersed in conscious breathing and mindful movement, you'll open the door to living a more conscious and empowered life.

Taming the Dragon

In order for the warrior to exit one gate and enter the next, he or she must tame the Dragon of the Gate he or she is leaving. In order to successfully tame the dragon, the warrior must undergo a personal transformation by surrendering some portion of his or her ego or "personal will" in order to glimpse a different level of perception and awareness.

Introduction: The Dragons of Transformation

As I mentioned before, in the Wu Ying Tao (formless way) martial art system there are four basic "Gates" of transformation: Blindness, Duality, Oneness and Emptiness. Each gate represents a level of skill and awareness that the student warrior has attained. The exit from each gate, which is simultaneously the entrance into the next, is "guarded" by a dragon. The ultimate goal is to consciously enter into a state of emptiness or "unconscious competence," where body and mind are unified in a harmonious state of conscious, creative flow.

In order for the warrior to exit one gate and enter the next, he or she must tame the Dragon of the Gate he or she is leaving. In order to successfully tame the dragon, the warrior must undergo a personal transformation by surrendering some portion of his or her ego or "personal will" in order to glimpse a different level of perception and awareness. The exit from the Gate of Blindness to the gate of Duality, for instance, is guarded by the Dragon of Sleep. While it's easy to remain in blindness, exiting this gate requires the student warrior to face his or her own ignorance, to look and listen.

FlowMotion™ can be an instrumental tool in your transformational toolbox if you allow yourself to become fully absorbed in the flow of each motion. While I will write in more detail about the Gates of Transformation in my next book, I do want to give some mention of them here.

The Gate of Blindness

When we blindly follow routines or unwittingly carry out senseless orders, we are acting like automations, with potentially grave consequences for ourselves and others.

— Ellen Langer, *Mindfulness,* page 4

The first gate or level of awareness and perception is the Gate of Blindness. The Gate of Blindness is the awareness-ability level called "unconscious incompetence." This is when you don't know how to do something and don't know that you don't know.

Unconscious incompetence is not a judgmental or pejorative term, it's a descriptive one used to describe the relationship between awareness and ability. Each time you master a new skill, such as FlowMotion™, your awareness and abilities co-develop together through the progression of unconscious incompetence at the Gate of Blindness, conscious incompetence at the Gate of Duality, conscious competence at the Gate of Oneness and unconscious (supra-conscious) competence at the Gate of Emptiness.

These gates or levels of awareness are not static or fixed. In fact, we continually transition from one gate of awareness into another as we engage in our daily activities; those activities in which we experience high levels of skill and awareness tend to be more enjoyable as we engage conscious competence at the Gate of Oneness or supra-conscious competence at the Gate of Emptiness, although this is usually a rare experience.

The Gate of Blindness is the starting point for learning FlowMotion™. It's important to remember that this is the first time you've done this exercise and there will be a tendency to "go to sleep" while practicing it. Particularly for trauma survivors, as you begin to reconnect with body memory through conscious breathing and mindful movement, there will be a tendency to "go unconscious" by dissociating from your in-your-body experience.

The Dragon of Sleep

The dragon guarding the exit to this gate is the Dragon of Sleep, which usually represents the part of ourselves that would rather remain unaware; it symbolizes the unconscious nature of the "severed-self." It manifests as physical numbness and disconnection, energy leaks and blocks, and chronic dissociation.

The Dragon of Sleep lives in the part of your body-mind where your conscious awareness will not go. It thrives upon those parts of yourself that you've split off and disowned. It consumes your pain and rage as food. Its purpose is to keep you locked into old, rigid, fixed beliefs, and emotional and behavioral patterns.

The Warrior Looks and Listens

In order to tame the Dragon of Sleep, the warrior must look and listen. Looking and listening are underutilized abilities. They're the abilities involved with suspending attention and judgment as you open yourself to new ideas, concepts, feelings, sensations, and emotions, to observe your ego "mindlessly" perceiving and reacting to stressful situations from (usually) unconscious and unexamined belief systems created in the past.

When you first begin FlowMotion™, be sensitive to old categories of thinking and perceiving that may appear. It's tempting to want to compare and classify your experience so that you can hang it somewhere within your already existing experiences. Release the temptation to do this. What you'll end up doing is immediately classifying the experience without fully experiencing it.

Also be sensitive to your habitual way of standing, breathing, walking, sitting, even your method of connecting your motions together. Your body is a wealth of information; continually bring your attention back, again and again, to sensing yourself inside your body. Who you are really is in your body; in many ways it is your body.

Allow yourself to fully, completely take in and absorb the experience of FlowMotion™, just as it is, without judgment or comparison. Whatever you experience while doing the form is exactly what you experience, nothing more or less. Let the experience be enough for that experience at that time. It will be different next time if you're willing to let go of the memory of your previous experience of how it was, or your anticipation about how it should be. Continue to bring your awareness back to the present moment, back into your body to simply observe and participate in what you're experiencing.

Some people I've taught have an immediate experience of flow the very first time they do FlowMotion™. Some don't. However, almost everybody feels an immediate sense of energy and rejuvenation. The most important concept to remember when starting out is to simply look and listen, let the experience be what it is without trying to capture, define or classify it. To define it is to confine it.

The Gate of Duality

The Gate of Duality represents "conscious incompetence," or when I know that I don't know. The awareness-ability level of conscious incompetence is where many student-warriors fail; you're conscious enough to be aware of your incompetence. This is that difficult stage toward mastering a skill in which your mind can see how it should be done, but your body seems to have an agenda of its own. No matter how much you struggle, your body just does not want to do what you tell it to do and this can cause you to feel foolish.

The Dragon of Fools

This can be a difficult gate for the student because the Dragon of Fools guards this gate. For the student that is not quite willing to learn, or hasn't committed to learning, this dragon can become a permanent barrier to learning and a reason for rebellion. Unwilling to seem foolish and unable, s/he returns to the Gate of Blindness where s/he doesn't have to deal with the inability.

— Professional Martial Arts Association: Instructors Handbook

The Dragon of Fools is a very difficult dragon to tame. It requires that you allow yourself to appear and feel foolish as you practice movements that at first can appear odd, even silly. When you're first learning the movements, trying to get them "right" can be very frustrating, particularly if you haven't consciously engaged your body for some period of time.

The Dragon of Fools manifests emotionally as the need to be right and the freezing fear of being humiliated. It often manifests as a divergent split in my ego-image; one part of me experiencing myself as superior and entitled, the other part of me feeling (secretly) shamed and devalued.

The Warrior is Humble

In order to tame the Dragon of Fools, the warrior must be humble, which is why so few people actually make it through this gate. Humility is the courageous willingness to align your self-image with your here and now, in the body, true and real experience. It requires accepting, owning, and transforming the part of you that you've split off, disowned, or frozen in body memory. Humility may be the most difficult state for the ego to achieve. To consciously surrender the control stick to another hand can both frighten and confuse us. Because we are so accustomed to being dominated by our ego-consciousness, it is very frightening to consider letting go of it.

At this level of skill and awareness you're fully aware that you don't completely know how to do the FlowMotion™ form, and it can become frustrating. This is the gate where your body feels as though it has a mind of its own. No matter how hard you try to get all of the movements done in the right time, with the right breath in the right way, it seems to elude you.

You've done the form enough to have most of the movements memorized and you've been practicing the visualization, but it still seems mechanical and uncoordinated. You can visualize in your mind how you want to look and feel, you just can't get your body to come along.

Welcome to the Gate of Duality, in this case, the duality of mind versus body. As your body-mind begins to awaken from its slumber, you become immediately aware that there has not been much dialogue between these two entities. This expresses itself as a lack of communication and coordination between head and body, a two-way communication and coordination. The body has as much to say as the head does when you begin to really look and listen.

Even though we spend so very little time consciously aware in the body, we expect to suddenly have a master-slave relationship in which the body does whatever we demand of it. I have some news for you: even though you haven't been consciously aware in your body for most of your life, that doesn't mean your body doesn't have a consciousness of its own, and that consciousness may have some different ideas about what your body will or won't do.

When practicing FlowMotion™, continually surrender your need for control over the movements. Once you've learned them well enough to do without thinking about them and there's a sense of continuity, release the idea that it's actually "you" doing the movements.

Allow the movements to begin to do themselves. You don't have to carry the burden of being in control by yourself. Relax, flow, and allow your body-mind to direct your movements. If you get confused in your head about how the movements should look or feel, return your attention to your center and your core. Do the movements in a way that feels as smooth, spontaneous, harmonious, and connected as they can be.

The Gate of Oneness

Your attention is not standing apart from your body, directing your actions, but is flowing along with the momentum. Your breath is flowing in and out exactly, according to the pace of your movements. Thus your body and all its parts, the attention, momentum and breath are all connected and flowing together as one unit. It is impossible for you to distinguish one part from the other within yourself; they all seem to be elements of one common force — chi.

— Bob Klein, *The Movements of Magic,* page 12

The Gate of Oneness is the awareness-skill level of conscious competence. This is the level of knowing how to do something well, as well as knowing how to know. You become efficient at the art of looking and listening and you're humble enough to be teachable. Your sense of self is becoming as strong, flexible, and resilient as your body.

You know you're entering the Gate of Oneness when your movements are smooth and coordinated and they flow with ease. Your body-mind becomes reflective and directive. You're able to simultaneously observe and participate fully in each motion. Your separate, individual body parts feel more connected and coordinated.

At the Gate of Oneness you've gained enough strength in your legs, knees, and back to do the FlowMotion™ form continuously for at least 10 minutes. When your body is able to move fluidly, continuously, and spontaneous for at least 10 minutes you'll become so absorbed in the activity that your awareness will merge with your actions.

What can begin to happen at the Gate of Oneness is a loss of the ego-centered perception and a glimpse of a different reality. This reality exists more in terms of sensation, emotion, and intuition than intellectual ideas. As you progressively experience the reality of your center and core, you begin to rely more on your heart and guts for direction and inspiration.

The Dragon of Distraction

Distraction can come in many different shapes and forms but can usually be traced back to the intrusion of some thought, sensation, feeling, or image that gets activated by the eruption of a traumatic (body) memory, causing you to instinctively physically recoil and become self-conscious.

When traumatic experiences are compartmentalized they're recorded as body memory; the emotion or energy of those experiences is also compartmentalized along with a conglomeration of thoughts, body sensations, and (partial) images. The longer you're able to do your form with continuous, mindful movement and conscious breathing, the "deeper" the body memory you access.

The Warrior is Focused

Being completely focused for any length of time is very difficult to do; it's not strenuous, it's difficult. In fact, the harder you try to focus, the more difficult it becomes. Like a correctly thrown punch, focus requires just the right amount of effort; too little will leave you unclear, too much will deplete you.

Thus your body and all its parts… all seem to be elements of one common force — chi.

— Bob Klein, *The Movements of Magic,* page 12

Being focused is the result of aligning who you are with what you're doing. It's completely surrendering to the activity at hand, mind and body focused in harmony. It's achieved by continually and consciously surrendering your ego-need for control, listening and spontaneously responding to the energy rhythms playing in your body.

As you progressively gain mastery over the movements of FlowMotion™, your body-mind becomes empowered to "take over" the reigns. The more you're able to surrender to and trust the awareness and ability of your Natural Self, the more you'll allow your body-mind to dance in the flow of spontaneous, creative *Energy* in *MOTION*.

The Gate of Emptiness

Moving meditation shows you that without mind, you can still function well. While you are active, the activity seems effortless because you aren't thinking your way through it. It just seems to happen by itself. This is 'not doing.' It is a feeling of joyful emptiness, the emptiness of the moon reflecting on a still lake.

— Bob Klein, *Movements of Magic,* page 17

The experience of emptiness is a glimpse into a different reality. The problem with these glimpses can be that they're very difficult to remember and put into words. That's because this is the awareness-ability level of unconscious or supra-conscious competence that resides in a place that operates outside the form of thoughts and words; it's truly the formless way.

Emptiness often reveals itself when you least suspect it. It will begin to manifest just outside your usual focus in the "corner of your eye;" the more you try to bring it into your focus, the more elusive it becomes. You can't deliberately make the experience of emptiness manifest, you can only create the conditions that will allow it to happen.

The conditions that are most conducive to the manifestation of Emptiness are a complete surrender, focus, and absorption into

your second to second, mind-body, physical, emotional, mental, and spiritual experience of FlowMotion™. Complete trust in, and willingness to spontaneously express, your deepest sense-feelings through breath, energy, and motion are also required to manifest the experience of emptiness.

There are times when doing FlowMotion™ where you'll feel that time actually is standing still. There's a part of you, your awareness, that's actually motionless while your body moves in perfect, fluid harmony.

Most remarkable is your perception. While you're taking in information through your eyes it seems as though you can actually "see" in a 360-degree circle. The place of your sight, however, isn't your eyes or your head. Instead, your "sight" seems to come from your Tan T'ien, your core.

There's also a very real sense of transparency that dissolves the boundary of inside versus outside. You have an almost palatable feeling that the energy you feel on the outside of your palms is the same, the very same energy, circulating through your core. Most of all, though, there's a sensation of dancing on energy, of flow, freedom, and creativity. As you continue to practice FlowMotion™, try to experience this sense of energy.

I hope that in reading this book and practicing these movements you've found some of the joy of FlowMotion™ and managed to transform some of the secondary trauma you may have stored into the vital, moving energy that is flow. Most of all, I hope you've come to some kind of understanding of your Natural Self. And if you haven't, that's fine too. Just remember: don't try to do these motions with forceful intensity, always trying to get them "right" or match them with the "correct way" you think you see in the DVD and illustrations. Relinquish the need to be right in the movements, the need to be right in life, the need to control every aspect of your internal energy. Relax into the movements. Experience the energy. Just be, right now. Enjoy yourself.

Bibliography:

Bennett-Goleman, Tara. *Emotional Alchemy*. Three Rivers Press. New York, New York. 2001.

Blackshaw, Lyn, Andrea Levy, and Janice Perciano. *Listening to High Utilizers of Mental Health Services: Recognizing, Responding to and Recovering from Trauma*. State of Oregon Mental Health and Developmental Disability Services Division. Salem, Oregon. 1999.

Bohm, David. *Wholeness and the Implicate Order*. Ark Paperbacks. New York, New York. 1990.

Calhoun, Patrick S., Jean C. Beckham, and Hayden B. Bosworth. "Caregiver Burden and Psychological Distress in Partners of Veterans with Chronic Post-Traumatic Stress Disorder," *The Journal of Traumatic Stress*. June 2002; Vol.15, Number 3.

Capra, Fritjof. *Uncommon Wisdom*. Harper Collins. Hammersmith, London. 1989.

Childre, Doc Lew. *Freeze Frame, Second Edition*. Planetary Books. Boulder Creek, California. 1998

Cohen, Kenneth. *The Way of Qigong: The Art and Science of Chinese Energy Healing*. Ballentine/Wellspring. New York, New York. 1997.

Crompton, Paul. *Chinese Soft Exercise*. Unwin Paperbacks. London. 1986.

Crum, Thomas. *The Magic of Conflict: Turning a Life of Work into a Work of Art*. Touchstone, Simon and Schuster Inc. New York, New York. 1997.

Csikszentmihalyi, Mihaly. *Finding Flow*. Basic Books. New York, New York. 1997.

Csikszentmihalyi, Mihaly. *The Evolving Self*. Harper Perennial. New York, New York. 1993.

Csikszentmihalyi, Mihaly. *Flow*. Harper Perennial. New York, New York. 1990.

Freud, Sigmund. *The Basic Writings of Sigmund Freud*. The Modern Library. New York, New York. 1938.

Gardner, Howard. *Multiple Intelligences*. Basic Books. New York, New York. 1993.

Goleman, Daniel. *Emotional Intelligence*. Bantam Books. New York, New York. 1995.

Herman, Judith. *Trauma and Recovery*. Basic Books. New York, New York. 1992.

Jacobson, Edith. *The Self and the Object World*. International Universities Press. New York, New York. 1977.

Keidel, Gladys Catkins. "Burnout and Compassion Fatigue Among Hospice Caregivers," *The American Journal of Hospice and Palliative Care*. May/June 2002; 19(3); 200-205.

Klein, Bob. *Movements of Magic: The Spirit of T'ai-Chi-Ch'uan, Second Edition*. Tai-chi-Ch'uan School. Sound Beach, New York. 1984.

Kohut, Heinz D. *The Analysis of the Self*. International Universities Press, Inc. New York, New York. 1977.

Kohut, Heinz D. *The Restoration of the Self*. International Universities Press, Inc. New York, New York. 1977.

Langer, Ellen. *Mindfulness*. Merloyd Lawrence Book, Addison-Wesley Publishing Company, Inc. New York, New York. 1989.

Levine, Peter. *Waking The Tiger: Healing Trauma*. North Atlantic Books. Berkley, California. 1997.

Loehr, Jim and Tony Swartz. *The Power of Full Engagement*. Free Press. New York, New York. 2003.

McCraty, Rollin, Mike Atkinson and Dana Tomasino. *Science of the Heart*. HeartMath Research Center. Boulder Creek, California. 2001.

Miller, Scott D., Mark Hubble, and Barry L. Duncan. *Handbook of Solution-Focused Brief Therapy*. Jossey-Bass Publishers. San Francisco, California. 1996.

Myss, Carolyn. *Anatomy of the Spirit*. Three Rivers Press. New York, New York. 1996.

Ornstein, Robert. *Multimind: A New Way of Looking at Human Behavior*. Houghton Mifflin Press. New York, New York. 1986.

Pearlman, Laurie Anne and Karen W. Saakvitne. *Trauma and the Therapist*. W.W. Norton & Co. New York, New York. 1995.

Pearsall, Paul. *The Heart's Code*. Broadway Books. New York, New York. 1998.

Pelletier, Kenneth R. *Mind as Healer, Mind as Slayer*. Delta–Bantam Doubleday Dell. New York, New York. 1977.

Pert, Candace. *Molecules of Emotion*. Touchstone Books. New York, New York. 1997.

Racker, Heinrich. *Transference and Counter-Transference*. International Universities Press. New York, New York. 1968.

Ravizza, Kenneth. "Increasing Awareness for Sport Performance," *Applied Sport Psychology: Personal Growth to Peak Performance*. Mayfield Publishing Co. Palo Alto, California. 1986

Rothschild, Babette. *The Body Remembers*. W.W. Norton & Co. New York, New York. 2000.

Russell, Peter. *Waking Up in Time*. Origin Press. Novato, California. 1998.

Saakvitne, Karen W. and Laurie Anne Pearlman. *Transforming the Pain*. W.W. Norton & Company. New York, New York. 1996.

Scaer, Robert. *The Body Bears The Burden: Trauma, Dissociation And Disease*. The Haworth Medical Press. Binghamton, New York. 2001.

Servan-Schreiber, David. *The Instinct to Heal*. Rodale. New York, New York. 2003.

Staff at People's Medical Publishing House. *The Chinese Way to a Long and Healthy Life*. Peoples Medical Publishing House. Beijing, China. 1988.

Stamm, B. Hudnall (Ed). *Secondary Traumatic Stress: Self-Care Issues for Clinicians, Researchers, and Educators; Second Edition*. Sidran Press. Lutherville, Maryland. 1988.

Stevens, José. *Transforming Your Dragons*. Bear & Company, Inc. Santa Fe, New Mexico. 1994.

Terrill, Bruce-and Jim Samuels. *Professional Martial Arts Instructors Handbook*. IMAA. Portland, Oregon. 1997.

Tolle, Eckhart. *Practicing the Power of Now*. New World Library — Namaste Publishing. Novato, California. 1999.

Van der Kolk, Bessel A., Alexander C. McFarlane, and Lars Weisaeth (Eds). *Traumatic Stress*. Guilford Press. New York, New York. 1996.

Vealey, Robin S. "Imagery Training for Performance Enhancement." *Applied Sport Psychology: Personal Growth to Peak Performance*. Mayfield Publishing Co. Palo Alto, California. 1986.

Zi, Nancy. *The Art of Breathing*. Bantam New Age Books. New York, New York. 1986.

Grateful acknowledgement is made for permission to reprint the following quotations:

From EMOTIONAL INTELLIGENCE by Daniel Goleman, copyright © 1995 by Daniel Goleman. Used by permission of Bantam Books, a division of Random House, Inc.

From MOVEMENTS OF MAGIC: THE SPIRIT OF T'AI-CHI-CH'UAN, Second Edition by Bob Klein, published by the Tai-chi-Chuan School, copyright © 1984. Reprinted by permission of Bob Klein.

From THE RESTORATION OF THE SELF by Heinz Kohut, published by International Universities Press, Inc., copyright © 1977.

From MINDFULNESS by Ellen Langer, copyright © 1989, published by Addison-Wesley Publishing Company, Inc. Reprinted by permission of Ellen Langer.

From WAKING THE TIGER: HEALING TRAUMA by Peter A. Levine, published by North Atlantic Books, copyright © 1997 by Peter A. Levine. Reprinted by permission of publisher.

From SCIENCE OF THE HEART by Rollin McCraty et. al., published by HeartMath Research Center, copyright © 2001.

From THE HEART'S CODE by Paul Pearsall, Ph. D., author of *The Last Self-Help Book You'll Ever Need*. Copyright © 1998, reprinted by permission of Paul Pearsall, Ph. D.

From MIND AS HEALER, MIND AS SLAYER by Kenneth R. Pelletier, Ph. D., copyright © 1977 by Kenneth R. Pelletier. Used by permission of Dell Publishing, a division of Random House, Inc.

Reprinted with permission of Simon & Schuster Touchstone Books division from MOLECULES OF EMOTION by Candace Pert. Copyright © 1997 by Candace Pert.

From WAKING UP IN TIME by Peter Russell, copyright © 1998, published by Origin Press. Reprinted by permission of Peter Russell.

From SECONDARY TRAUMATIC STRESS: SELF-CARE ISSUES FOR CLINICIANS, RESEARCHERS, AND EDUCATORS; Second Edition by B. Hudnall Stamm (Ed), copyright © 1995, 1999. Reprinted courtesy of Sidran Institute Press.

Excerpted from PRACTICING THE POWER OF NOW by Eckhart Tolle, published by New World Library/ www.newworldlibrary.com and Namaste Publishing/www.namaste publishing.com copyright © 1999. Used by permission of Namaste Publishing.

From TRAUMATIC STRESS by Bessel A. Van der Kolk, Alexander C. McFarlane, and Lars Weisaeth (Eds), copyright © 1996. Reprinted by permission of The Guilford Press.

From "Imagery Training for Performance Enhancement" by Robin S. Vealey, in APPLIED SPORT PSYCHOLOGY; PERSONAL GROWTH TO PEAK PERFORMANCE, published by Mayfield Publishing Company, copyright © 1986. Reprinted by permission of Robin S. Vealey.

Breath of relief Products

Karl LaRowe has developed CD, DVD, and VHS recordings that illustrate various aspects of relaxation, from Qigong exercises to body awareness and FlowMotion™. These can be purchased from Karl's web site, **www.BreathofRelief.com.**

To book for Karl for speaking engagements of for more information on him and his services, please visit his web site: www.BreathofRelief.com

Body Awareness | CD

This is a 19 minute relaxation/visualization audio CD developed specifically for patients with post traumatic stress disorder, care providers with secondary post traumatic stress disorder, and others suffering from trauma-related symptoms. In this guided visualization, each body part is awakened, energized, and relaxed using dynamic tension, measured breathing, and centering exercises.

The Art of FlowMotion™ | DVD & VHS

FlowMotion™ is a set of simple, easy to learn continous flowing exercises that channel stress into positive energy. It harmonizes the mind and body with the breath.

Qigong for Care Providers | DVD & VHS

Qigong (pronounced Chi-Gong), is an ancient Chinese martial arts used to harmonize breath, energy, and motion. It was developed specifically to help health care professionals transform Compassion Fatigue into flow and peak performance. This 20 minute production was filmed in Singapore with martial arts master Simon Yong.

Caring for Care Providers

This is a home study course for all care providers who are experiencing compassion fatigue — or secondary trauma. It is authorized by the Oregon Board of Clinical of Social Workers for six hours of continuing education.

Workshops and Seminars

There are a million ways to relieve stress, but nothing gets the mind and body grooving together quite like FlowMotion™. Developed from the ancient Chinese practice of Qigong, FlowMotion™ has helped thousands attain a heightened sense of self-awareness and stillness rarely offered by other forms of meditation.

Karl LaRowe is available to present dynamic, full day FlowMotion™ workshops to groups, organizations, and businesses whose members may be facing burnout. If you're serious about empowering your people to manage Compassion Fatigue before it leads to burnout, please give Karl a call. To find the service that's right for your group, visit Karl on the web at www.BreathofRelief.com.

Tip of the Month

Combat Compassion Fatigue. Sign up for Karl LaRowe's regular e-mail tip of the month at www.BreathofRelief.com. The most effective and up to date techniques to alleviate job stress from the English-speaking world's leading authority on Compassion Fatigue are just a few clicks away.